The Emergency Market Mapping and Analysis Toolkit

Praise for the book ...

'The IFRC has been proud to support the development of the EMMA toolkit and recognizes the value it brings to improving post disaster needs assessment – helping us to meet our strategic aim to save lives, protect livelihoods and prepare for, and recover from, disasters and crises.

EMMA is becoming an important part of our detailed assessments in the first weeks following major disasters – informing a holistic and integrated approach to disaster response and early recovery. EMMA techniques help to determine appropriate response interventions, to promote greater choice for disaster affected populations, and to reduce the risk of aid dependency. Particularly useful are Market and Response Analysis (market maps and options and recommendation framework).'

Simon Eccleshall, Head, Disaster Services Department,
International Federation of the Red Cross and Red Crescent Societies

'In the past several years, there has been increasing collaboration between market development practitioners and emergency response practitioners. This collaboration is to be greatly celebrated and encouraged and the EMMA manual is one excellent result of this collaboration. For too long humanitarian relief which aimed to 'lay the ground work' for economic development did nothing of the sort. And, market development practitioners would follow and try to correct the many market distortions that had been created. The net result was very limited, if any, progress for the communities we are there to serve.

Evidence from microfinance has shown that we can and should start early after an emergency or other crisis to do it right from the beginning. Congratulations to IRC and the other agencies that have the foresight and tenacity to make this happen.'

Mayada El-Zoghbi, Senior Microfinance Specialist, CGAP, World Bank

'The EMMA toolkit effectively brings comprehensive market analysis approaches to the rapid emergency context. It's a critical step forward in improving economic development practices in crisis contexts.'

Timothy H. Nourse, Chief of Party, Expanded and Sustained Access to Financial
Services (ESAF) Program, Academy for Educational Development, Ramallah, West Bank

'EMMA is a clear and accessible framework for analyzing complex crisis situations from the perspective of disruptions in market systems, and for designing and implementing interventions based on basic market principles. It pushes relief and recovery programming to prioritize preserving and rebuilding market structures and create longer term opportunities for economic stability and security. The tool bridges a gap between the relief and development fields by creating a common vocabulary and vision around facilitating the transition to sustainable economic recovery and growth.'

Adina Saperstein, Associate, Enterprise Development Practice Manager,
Banyan Global

The Emergency Market Mapping and Analysis Toolkit

Mike Albu

PRACTICAL ACTION
Publishing

Practical Action Publishing Ltd
Schumacher Centre for Technology and Development
Bourton on Dunsmore, Rugby,
Warwickshire, CV23 9QZ, UK
www.practicalactionpublishing.org

ISBN 978 1 85339 699 1

This Toolkit is made possible by the generous support of the American people
through the United States Agency for International Development (USAID). The
contents are the responsibility of Oxfam, IRC, and Practical Action Publishing and
do not necessarily reflect the views of USAID or the United States Government.

Since 1974, Practical Action Publishing (formerly Intermediate Technology
Publications and ITDG Publishing) has published and disseminated books and
information in support of international development work throughout the world.
Practical Action Publishing is a trading name of Practical Action Publishing Ltd
(Company Reg. No. 1159018), the wholly owned publishing company of
Practical Action. Practical Action Publishing trades only in support of its parent
charity objectives and any profits are covenanted back to Practical Action
(Charity Reg. No. 247257, Group VAT Registration No. 880 9924 76).

Cover photo: EMMA team in Myanmar mapping the fishing net market.
Credit: Anita Auerbach
Cover design by Practical Action Publishing
Indexed by Andrea Palmer
Typeset by S.J.I. Services
Printed by Hobbs The Printers

Contents

Boxes

Introduction

Step 1

Step 2

Step 3

Step 4

Step 5

Step 6

Step 7

Step 8

Step 9

Step 10

Acknowledgements

The EMMA toolkit was developed with the advice and contributions of many committed individuals and agencies. The market-system concepts and mapping tool were originally developed with colleagues at Practical Action, especially Alison Griffith. Applying these tools to humanitarian emergency contexts was an innovation of Pantaleo Creti.

I am especially grateful to Emmet Murphy, who worked tirelessly with me to research the market analysis needs and capabilities of humanitarian agencies. He wrote much of the earliest draft of the toolkit with me, and contributed hugely to the content from which EMMA eventually evolved. Emmet also helped organize, in difficult circumstances, the pilot study that later took place in Haiti.

Anita Auerbach and Dee Goluba also both made major contributions to the revision and development of EMMA through their leadership of the piloting process in Kenya, Haiti, Myanmar and Pakistan. Their experience, enthusiasm, perseverance and capacity for reflection were invaluable. I am truly indebted to them both.

I would like to thank the initial informants to this process, who included Tanya Boudreau, Carol Ward, David Bright, Laura Hammond, Patricia Bonnard, Cynthia Donovan, Tracy Gerstle, Josephine Hutton, Richard Acaye, Leo Nalugon, Roman Majcher, Frederic Vignoud, Robert Tabana, Silke Pietzsch, Sophie Dunn, Thabani Maphosa, Mary Morgan, Jennifer Nyberg, and David Rinck.

Development of the toolkit, through various stages, would not have been possible without the generous support of InterAction, OFDA, Oxfam and the Waterloo Foundation. Detailed comments and constructive criticism from many experienced advisors was vital to this process, and I would especially like to thank Heloise Troc, Lesley Adams, Camilla Knox-Peebles, Lili Mohiddin, Mary Atkinson, Paul Harvey, Nana Skau, Karri Goldner Byrne and Jonathan Brass.

The pilot exercises depended entirely on the generous cooperation of many humanitarian agencies, including International Rescue Committee, Oxfam GB, Mercy Corps, World Food Program, Save the Children UK, Haitian Red Cross, Canadian Red Cross, CHF International, ACDI/VOCA, Famine Early Warning System Network, Oxfam Quebec, and Oxfam Novib.

Many individuals gave their time and energy to the piloting process, and it is almost unfair to name a few – but I would especially like to thank Lili Mohiddin, Karri Goldner Byrne, Vivien Knipps, Marc Theuss, Mike Leung, Nway Nway Soe and Mg Myo Min, Kate Montgomery, Rick Bauer, and Tony Stitt.

Finally, I want to thank my partner Kate and son Billy for their love, support and patience during this project. EMMA was conceived and delivered at around the same time as our gorgeous daughter Evie, to whom this publication is dedicated.

PART ONE
INTRODUCTION

The EMMA toolkit: introduction and overview

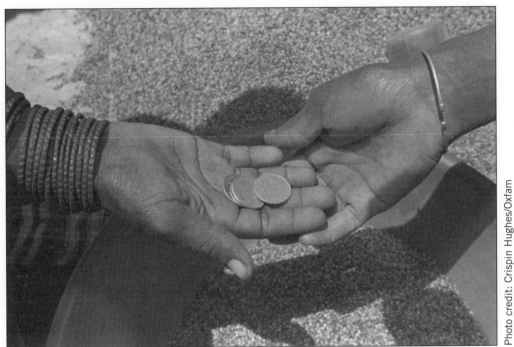

Paying for sorghum at a market stall, Uganda

0.1 Introduction

In recent years, international humanitarian agencies have been adapting their responses to emergencies. Many have begun using cash-based initiatives, alongside or in place of conventional relief distributions of food and non-food items. Local procurement is also being encouraged, and opportunities for other innovative responses explored (Harvey 2005, 2007).

These changes in practice draw attention to the need for better analysis of markets. There is a growing realization that the best opportunities for assisting women and men may be missed unless emergency responses are designed with a good understanding of critical market systems. Moreover, lack of this market analysis in humanitarian programmes may be damaging the livelihoods, jobs, and businesses upon which people's long-term security depends.

Markets are a crucial component of how people survive. So understanding how they are functioning and disrupted is critical to any analysis of hunger, and vulnerability to food and livelihood insecurity or poverty.

Paul Harvey, Humanitarian Policy Group, ODI

> **Box 0.1 What is a 'market system'?**
>
> A market system is a network of producers, suppliers, processors, traders, buyers, and consumers that are all involved in producing, exchanging, and consuming a particular item or service. The system includes various forms of infrastructure, input providers, and services. And it operates within the context of rules and norms that shape this system's particular business environment.

Market systems matter in emergencies

Market systems play a vital role in supplying critical goods or services to ensure survival and protect livelihoods, both in the immediate aftermath of a disaster and in the longer term. Before, during, and beyond any crisis, emergency-affected women and men also depend on market systems as sources of income and remuneration.

Box 0.2 Why market systems matter in emergencies

For ensuring survival	For protecting livelihoods	
Market systems may be able to provide affected target groups with food, essential household items, fuel, and other forms of relief or services to meet basic needs	Market systems may be able to provide affected target groups with urgently needed tools, agricultural inputs and services, and fodder and fuel, or replace other livelihood assets	Market systems may be able to provide affected target groups with jobs and opportunities for wage labour, or link them to buyers for their produce

The rationale for EMMA is that a better understanding of the most critical market systems in an emergency situation enables humanitarian agencies to consider a broader range of responses.

As well as conventional in-kind distributions and cash-based interventions, these response options can include local procurement and other innovative forms of market-system support that enable humanitarian programmes to make better use of existing market actors' capabilities, while understanding the risks.

The results of using EMMA therefore are:

- more efficient use of humanitarian resources;
- less risk of prolonged dependency on outside assistance;
- encouragement for the transition to economic recovery.

Gender and market systems

People's relationships with other actors in market systems (i.e. traders, employers, buyers) are shaped by issues of power – which often have gender, class, or ethnic dimensions. We cannot assume that the roles and responsibilities of women and men, and hence their market needs, are the same. EMMA explicitly deals with these differences in its selection of target groups (section 1.6), and deals with power as a component of the market environment in market-system mapping (section 0.11).

0.2 EMMA: what, why, who, and when?

WHAT is the EMMA toolkit?

EMMA is a set of tools (this toolkit) and guidance notes (the reference manual on CD-ROM). It encourages and assists front-line humanitarian staff in sudden-onset emergencies to better understand, accommodate, and make use of market systems. It does not offer a simplistic blue-print for action. However, EMMA does provide accessible, relevant guidance to staff who are not already specialists in market analysis.

Box 0.3 The essential scope of EMMA	
Sudden-onset emergencies	where fast-moving events mean that agencies have little advance knowledge of markets and limited resources to investigate them
A broad range of needs	any market system that may be critical in addressing priority needs, including food, non-food items, and other services
Rapid decision-making	supporting humanitarian teams to take urgent-response decisions faced in the first few weeks of a crisis

The EMMA toolkit adds value to established humanitarian practices in diverse contexts. EMMA tools are adaptable, rough-and-ready, speed-orientated processes designed to reflect the information constraints and urgency of decision making required in the first few weeks of a sudden-onset emergency situation. The EMMA process is therefore intended to be integrated flexibly into different organizations' emergency-response planning.

Although designed with sudden-onset situations in mind, EMMA is also likely to be valuable for staff planning for the transition into the early recovery phase of programming.

WHY use EMMA?

EMMA's aim is to improve the effectiveness and efficiency of early humanitarian actions taken to ensure people's survival; to protect their food security and their livelihoods; and to help agencies to avoid doing harm. EMMA helps front-line staff to both *understand* the important market aspects of an emergency situation that may not otherwise be considered adequately or early enough; and *communicate* this knowledge promptly and effectively into programme decision-making processes.

Six reasons why EMMA is valuable:

1. *To make early decisions about the wisdom of different direct-response options.* EMMA compares the likely outcomes and risks of different types of direct intervention (see Box 0.5) to decide which forms (or combinations) are most appropriate in meeting people's priority needs.

2.   *To assess opportunities for complementary 'indirect' actions.*
     EMMA explores opportunities for alternative indirect forms of market support
     (see Box 0.5) that can rehabilitate or assist recovery of critical market systems.

3.   *To reduce the risk of doing harm.*
     EMMA increases awareness of the potential to harm businesses and
     households in critical market systems. Hence it can reduce aid dependency,
     promote long-term recovery, and increase the stability of local markets that
     provide people with goods, services, and sources of income.

4.   *To assist in monitoring the performance and accessibility of market systems.*
     EMMA profiles can help agencies to track both the continuing impact of a
     crisis, and the outcomes of humanitarian actions, on critical market systems.
     Up-to-date information about market access and performance can alert
     managers to any adverse effects of humanitarian actions, and enable them
     to make appropriate decisions about when and how to phase out assistance.

5.   *To improve the quality of disaster preparedness.*
     Through better knowledge of how critical market systems work, their
     potentials and vulnerabilities, EMMA market maps and profiles can improve
     the quality of disaster-preparedness planning.

6.   *To define the requirements for more detailed market analysis.*
     Where information is poor, time is short, and skills to interpret market
     data are weak, EMMA can still help managers to define detailed terms of
     reference for more thorough research of particularly critical market systems.

Box 0.4 Risks of doing harm via markets

Emergencies often cause damage to market functions and trade networks. This
can be made worse by inappropriate humanitarian responses. For example:
*   prolonged in-kind relief may aggravate the natural depression of a local
     economy caused by people's loss of income in an emergency;
*   ill-considered cash-transfers may intensify the natural inflationary price
     rises caused by local shortages of essential goods in an emergency.

Box 0.5 What are 'direct' and 'indirect' responses?

Direct responses	Indirect responses ('market-system support')
Actions that directly assist emergency-affected populations • Distributions of food or goods • Cash or voucher distributions • Cash-for-Work, Food-for-Work programmes • Provision of shelter, water, or sanitation • Nutrition programmes	Actions with others – e.g. traders, officials, policy makers – to benefit affected populations indirectly • Rehabilitation of key infrastructure, transport links, bridges, etc. • Grants (or loans) for local businesses to restore stocks, rehabilitate premises, or repair vehicles • Provision of technical expertise to local businesses, employers, or service providers

Box 0.6 Examples of the value added by EMMA

Comparing different direct-response options: cash vs. in-kind distributions

- A major flood event destroys the standing crops and food stocks of half a million people in a region that is not accustomed to such disasters. Immediately, humanitarian agencies begin household-level distribution of standard food rations e.g. rice, lentils, oil, sugar. Local traders appear to be quite resilient, however, and staple foods, including some local produce, are soon on sale. It is not clear to what extent this market-based supply can meet the target population's needs. EMMA can help agencies to decide whether and when it is safe to switch to cash-based assistance.

- A severe earthquake damages the homes and possessions of two million residents in a mountainous region. Winter is approaching, and many lack adequate clothing and blankets. Donated garments are easily available from some donors, but most are culturally inappropriate. Meanwhile, on the plains below, clothing factories, part of a well-functioning garments market system, are undamaged. EMMA can explore the relative advantages of local procurement, or cash, to meet people's needs.

Exploring opportunities for complementary 'indirect' actions: market-system support

- Coastal paddy-fields have been wrecked by salt-water intrusion following a cyclone. Rehabilitation will require extensive, deep ploughing of the soil – at a time when the local population is struggling to reconstruct homes and infrastructure. An agency considers buying and distributing power tillers to farmers but is concerned about the cost, sustainability, and social impact of this action. EMMA can investigate the sector and reveal any opportunities for strengthening the local rental market for agri-machines instead – for example, by using vouchers for farmers, and loans to rental-service providers.

Avoiding doing harm

- After the 2004 Asian tsunami, humanitarian agencies got involved in purchasing and distributing fishing boats on a huge scale. Unfortunately, in many locations there was inadequate analysis of the complex social relations linking fishing households, boat ownership, and the fish market system. As a result, in many places too many boats, or the wrong types of boat, were distributed. This led to over-fishing when the demand for fish was still low, to fishing yields that could not be ecologically sustained, and to worsening social tensions that affected vulnerable groups. In such situations, EMMA can provide insight into the risks and help agencies to avoid the worst mistakes.

WHO is EMMA for?

EMMA is for members of staff leading early assessments on the front line during sudden-onset emergencies, and during the transition to early recovery programming. By extension, EMMA is also for their managers and for decision makers responsible for planning initial and early responses to crisis.

EMMA is designed for generalists, as well as staff specializing in food-security, shelter, water, and sanitation sectors. This includes both front-line international support personnel drafted into a major emergency situation, and experienced local or national staff who may have good knowledge of livelihoods and economy in the affected area.

EMMA assumes limited previous experience of economic or market analysis. For this reason, EMMA tries to avoid technical language, or tools which require refined quantitative skills. However, those who conduct and lead EMMA processes – alone or with a small team – will greatly benefit from a pragmatic capacity to organize assessments flexibly, to reflect on information, and to think analytically.

EMMA is, in effect, an emergency stop-gap process: a pragmatic response to the typical human-resource limitations and shortages of information that constrain efforts to address market-related issues in sudden-onset emergency situations. By implication, it is less relevant for professional economists or market specialists who aim to conduct more thorough analysis of market systems, food security, or economic rehabilitation needs – for example in recovery phases of emergencies.

WHEN to use EMMA?

EMMA aims to encourage speedy, rough-and-ready market-system analysis during the first few weeks of an emergency situation. It is designed for use in rapid-onset emergency situations...
* when background information is limited;
* when time and capacity to analyse existing markets are limited;
* when expert market-analysis capabilities are not yet available.

EMMA is not relevant to rapid assessments and initial concept notes in the first few days of a crisis. It can be used, however, as soon as an emergency situation has begun to stabilize. This is so that the findings are not in danger of becoming immediately out of date due to further changes as the situation evolves.

Typically, this means that EMMA is used:
* once absolute priority needs (survival) are already being addressed;
* once displaced people have settled, at least temporarily;
* once market actors (e.g. producers, retailers, traders) have had a chance to assess their own situation and begin devising coping strategies

This means that if suitable personnel are available, EMMA can potentially be used within two weeks of the onset of an emergency. However, it will often take rather longer.

EMMA may continue to be useful for many weeks (or even months) into a crisis, if humanitarian agencies' understanding of key market systems that relate to emergency needs remains sketchy, or if changing market conditions need to be monitored. It may be valuable for early-recovery programming if more rigorous market analysis is not feasible.

In practice, the timing of EMMA will depend on reconciling the information and decision-making needs of the organization that is using the toolkit with the availability of staff to conduct these exercises.

0.3 EMMA and market systems

The 'market system' is a fundamental concept in EMMA. A market system is the entire web of people, businesses, structures, and rules that are involved in producing, trading, and consuming any product or service. The market system determines how a product or service is accessed, produced, exchanged, and made available to different people. This concept is best explained and revealed by using an example of a market-system map (see Box 0.7).

Box 0.7 Baseline market map – 'beans' example from Haiti

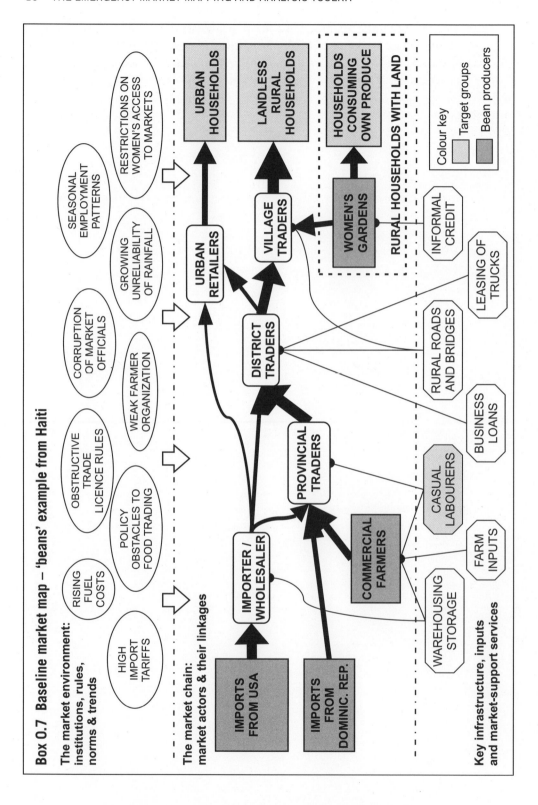

The market environment: institutions, rules, norms & trends

HIGH IMPORT TARIFFS

RISING FUEL COSTS

POLICY OBSTACLES TO FOOD TRADING

OBSTRUCTIVE TRADE LICENCE RULES

CORRUPTION OF MARKET OFFICIALS

WEAK FARMER ORGANIZATION

SEASONAL EMPLOYMENT PATTERNS

GROWING UNRELIABILITY OF RAINFALL

RESTRICTIONS ON WOMEN'S ACCESS TO MARKETS

The market chain: market actors & their linkages

URBAN HOUSEHOLDS

LANDLESS RURAL HOUSEHOLDS

HOUSEHOLDS CONSUMING OWN PRODUCE

URBAN RETAILERS

VILLAGE TRADERS

WOMEN'S GARDENS

RURAL HOUSEHOLDS WITH LAND

DISTRICT TRADERS

PROVINCIAL TRADERS

COMMERCIAL FARMERS

IMPORTER / WHOLESALER

IMPORTS FROM USA

IMPORTS FROM DOMINIC. REP.

Key infrastructure, inputs and market-support services

WAREHOUSING STORAGE

FARM INPUTS

BUSINESS LOANS

RURAL ROADS AND BRIDGES

LEASING OF TRUCKS

INFORMAL CREDIT

CASUAL LABOURERS

Colour key

Target groups

Bean producers

Mapping is one of the main tools in EMMA. Market-system maps, and other tools such as seasonal calendars, are at the heart of EMMA. Research and interviews with all sorts of different market actors and other informants are used to rapidly draw up comprehensive pictures of the system. These maps capture the most relevant available information and enable comparisons to be made between pre-crisis and emergency-affected situations. They are also vital tools for communicating EMMA findings and recommendations to busy decision makers.

EMMA and market-system selection

EMMA investigates market systems for different items separately. As the example in Box 0.7 illustrates, every crop, non-food item, or service has its own particular market system. This means that it is necessary to decide early in the EMMA process (Step 2) which market systems – i.e. which items, crops, products – are critical from the humanitarian perspective.

The need to focus on particular market systems is not a huge obstacle to using EMMA in practice. Although EMMA analyses every market system independently of every other system, it is perfectly feasible to conduct fieldwork for two or more EMMA studies simultaneously. Also, some commodities may have such similar market systems that it is feasible to use one as a proxy for others. For example, essential household items that are imported from outside the disaster area may come along very similar supply chains.

0.4 Overview of EMMA – the three strands

The EMMA process has three basic strands, represented by the strap-line '*People, Markets, Emergency Response*'.

Initially, the strands are relatively separate, like parallel lines of enquiry in an investigation. However, as EMMA proceeds, these strands should knit together like a rope, providing a strong, coherent analysis to support the weight of your final recommendations (see Box 0.8).

Box 0.8 Three strands of EMMA

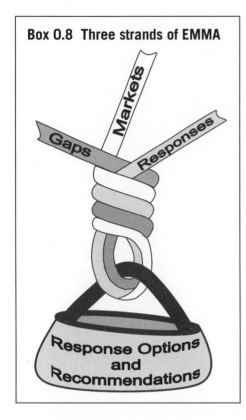

A. Gap analysis ('people') strand

This strand is about understanding the emergency situation, priority needs, and preferences of those most affected by the emergency: our target population. It also puts these households' needs (the gaps in their resources) in the context of their economic profile and livelihood strategies.

B. Market-analysis strand

This strand is about understanding each critical market system in terms of its constraints and capabilities to play a role in the emergency response. It develops a map and profile of the pre-crisis baseline situation and explores the impact of the emergency on it.

C. Response-analysis strand

This strand is about exploring different options and opportunities for humanitarian agencies. It looks at each option's respective feasibility, likely outcomes, benefits, and risks, before leading to recommendations for action.

The three strands run throughout the EMMA process, supporting each other, as follows.

The results of the gap analysis inform the market-system analysis by defining what the market system has to achieve if it is to meet people's needs. These results also contribute to the response analysis, for example by describing women's and men's preferred forms of assistance (see Box 0.9).

Box 0.9 Results of gap analysis – example

25,000 households in a disaster area are normally food-secure in terms of locally grown rice at this time of year. Due to 60 per cent flood destruction of the current crop, they face a total collective shortfall (gap) of 1200 MT / month until the next harvest in nine months. Both women and men in the target population have a strong preference for cash-based assistance. For women this is mainly because they are concerned about the probable type and quality of food aid; whereas men favour cash because it is flexible.

The results of the market-system analysis inform the response analysis by assessing what the market system is capable of delivering, and by identifying the main constraints that it faces (see Box 0.10). Early market-analysis findings may also support the gap-analysis process by highlighting issues that require field investigation, for example market-access constraints of which the target population are unaware.

Box 0.10 Results of market-system analysis – example

Traders in the disaster area will struggle to supply an extra 1200 MT rice / month from local stocks, and are not accustomed to 'importing' more than 300 MT / month (baseline). The main obstacles to efforts to increase supplies are lack of finance (trading capital), and damage to the local fleet of trucks. In addition, many rural feeder roads to remoter villages are blocked. However, rice traders in the nearest large city have ample supplies (baseline 4000 MT / month).

The response-analysis results inform the final conclusions and recommendations of EMMA, by evaluating feasibility, risks, advantages, and disadvantages of the response options or combinations of options identified during the EMMA process (see Box 0.11).

Box 0.11 Results of response analysis – example

Response option	Timing	Benefits	Risks	Indicators
Local procurement, with agency distribution	Start in 2–3 weeks	Rapid, operationally feasible response.	May drive away local rice traders. Increased long-term dependency.	Prices. Level of trade activity
Household vouchers, plus loans and transport assistance for local traders	Start in 4–5 weeks	Women prefer vouchers. Less costly. Boost for local economy.	Complex to administer. Risk of corruption. Donor scepticism.	Prices. Voucher redemption
Cash for Work, clearing rural feeder roads	Start in 1–2 weeks	Reduced transport costs and prices. Boost for local economy.	May divert labour from key agricultural activities. May exclude extremely vulnerable individuals.	Labour rates. Social exclusion.

Early response-analysis findings also contribute to the gap analysis and market-system analysis processes, by indicating a variety of feasible options and narrowing the scope of EMMA fieldwork so that interviews can focus on gathering the most useful information.

0.5 The EMMA process – ten steps

The EMMA process can be divided into ten steps, covering the general sequence of activities. However, EMMA is also an iterative process. In practice, activities in different steps will overlap, and we may return to particular steps repeatedly, as our analysis of each market system is revised. This continues until a 'good-enough' final picture is achieved.

Box 0.12 Ten steps in EMMA	
1. *Essential preparation*	Do background research and in-country briefings; consult on the agency mandate, terms of reference and practicalities; identify target population and their priority needs
2. *Market selection*	Select the most critical market systems for EMMA to study, using various specific criteria; and then identify the key analytical questions that will guide the investigation of each system
3. *Preliminary analysis*	Draft initial provisional household profiles, seasonal calendars, baseline and emergency-affected maps of the market system; and then identify key informants and useful leads for fieldwork
4. *Fieldwork preparation*	Agree and set the fieldwork agenda; devise the questionnaires, interview plans and information-recording formats needed for EMMA interviews and other fieldwork
5. *Fieldwork activities*	Conduct fieldwork activities: interviews and other information gathering; this section includes guidance on interview methods and tips relating to different categories of informant
6. *Mapping the market*	Produce final versions of baseline and emergency market maps, as well as seasonal calendars and household profiles that describe the situation, and will inform the three 'analytical' steps that follow
7. *Gap analysis*	Finalize the gap analysis strand: use household profiles, information on priority needs, shortfalls and access constraints in order to finally estimate the total gap which needs to be addressed
8. *Market analysis*	Complete the market analysis strand: use market maps and data to analyse availability, conduct, performance and thus estimate the capacity of the market system to meet the gap
9. *Response analysis*	Finish the response analysis strand: make reasoned recommendations, based on the market system logic, feasibility, timing and risks of different options, including cash, in-kind relief or other market support
10. *Communicate results*	Consult with colleagues, and communicate EMMA's results to wider audiences (donors, agencies); using concise briefings and eye-catching map-based presentations and reports

The way in which these three parallel strands and the ten consecutive steps are interrelated is represented in the flow-chart in Box 0.13.

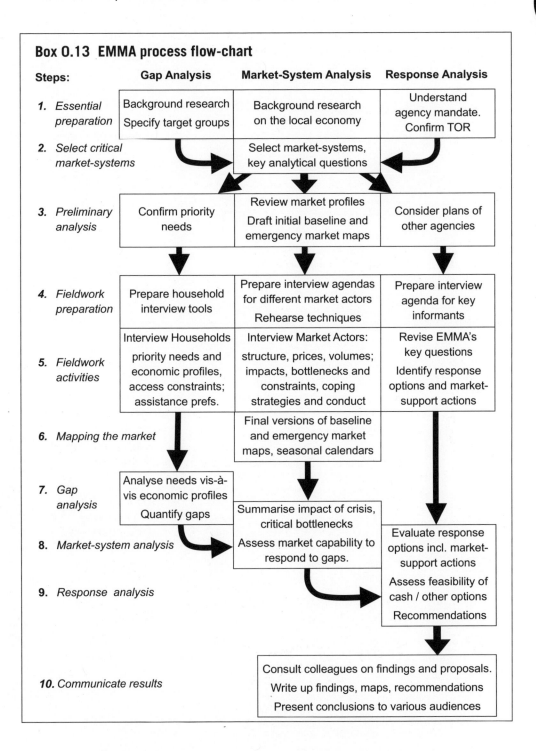

Box 0.13 EMMA process flow-chart

Steps:	Gap Analysis	Market-System Analysis	Response Analysis
1. *Essential preparation*	Background research Specify target groups	Background research on the local economy	Understand agency mandate. Confirm TOR
2. *Select critical market-systems*		Select market-systems, key analytical questions	
3. *Preliminary analysis*	Confirm priority needs	Review market profiles Draft initial baseline and emergency market maps	Consider plans of other agencies
4. *Fieldwork preparation*	Prepare household interview tools	Prepare interview agendas for different market actors Rehearse techniques	Prepare interview agenda for key informants
5. *Fieldwork activities*	Interview Households priority needs and economic profiles, access constraints; assistance prefs.	Interview Market Actors: structure, prices, volumes; impacts, bottlenecks and constraints, coping strategies and conduct	Revise EMMA's key questions Identify response options and market-support actions
6. *Mapping the market*		Final versions of baseline and emergency market maps, seasonal calendars	
7. *Gap analysis*	Analyse needs vis-à-vis economic profiles Quantify gaps		
8. *Market-system analysis*		Summarise impact of crisis, critical bottlenecks Assess market capability to respond to gaps.	Evaluate response options incl. market-support actions
9. *Response analysis*			Assess feasibility of cash / other options Recommendations
10. *Communicate results*		Consult colleagues on findings and proposals. Write up findings, maps, recommendations Present conclusions to various audiences	

0.6 EMMA's principles

EMMA builds on what humanitarian agencies already do.
- EMMA is a flexible process, with a few clearly defined tools, which is intended to be adapted to each situation and each agency's ways of working.

EMMA is not just business-as-usual: it asks humanitarian staff to think differently.
- EMMA draws attention to the importance of market systems that are critical to meeting affected populations' priority needs, both now and in the longer term.
- EMMA may lead agencies to consider unconventional kinds of response, including 'indirect' actions to rehabilitate or support damaged market systems.

EMMA is for non-specialists to enable them to make urgent decisions that are 'adequate for purpose'.
- EMMA is mostly qualitative rather than quantitative.
- EMMA is intended to assist early decision making in the first weeks of a crisis, looking forward up to one year ahead. It does not provide the detailed analysis ideally required for long-term programming.

EMMA does not put markets before people.
- EMMA is about making markets work for women and men in emergencies. Most crisis-affected households were involved in market systems before the crisis occurred: perhaps for acquiring food, essential items, and services, or for selling products (e.g. crops) and labour.
- In the EMMA process, understanding the market system for an item like rice therefore includes not just the retailers and millers who trade in rice, but also farmers and agricultural labourers (who may be men), suppliers of seeds and inputs, and of course rice consumers (who may be women).

EMMA has a livelihoods perspective.
- EMMA differentiates between different livelihoods and social groups, recognising that men's and women's normal livelihood strategies shape their relationships with market systems, their coping strategies, and their different needs in an emergency.
- Gender roles, ethnicity, wealth rank, health status, disability, etc. may all be important factors affecting people's access to and engagement with market systems, their coping strategies, and needs.

EMMA allows you to integrate existing and relevant information from different sources:
- household surveys, trader interviews, official statistics, market profiles, and other literature.

EMMA encourages optimal ignorance and appropriate imprecision.
- EMMA is about rapid, rough and ready, good-enough analysis. Both the amount of information and the details required to produce useful findings

in a limited period of time are kept to a minimum. EMMA encourages users to disregard non-essential or unnecessary detail ('optimal ignorance') and be satisfied with approximations and rough estimates ('appropriate imprecision').

EMMA is an iterative process.
*   EMMA starts with rough approximate ideas about the market system and then, by gradually incorporating new information gathered from interviews and fieldwork, repeatedly revises and refines the picture until a 'good-enough' analysis is achieved.

EMMA's relationship with other assessments.
*   Much of the Gap Analysis strand is similar to emergency needs assessments, especially rapid integrated appraisals. However, EMMA looks more specifically at target households' interactions with markets – in order to understand which market systems are critical to different livelihood groups, and how access to them has been affected by the emergency.

0.7 Timetable for EMMA in practice

EMMA can take between two and four weeks to implement. Variables include the context and the scale of the emergency. It also depends on resources: the number of market systems to be studied and the number of staff used. Other factors include how well members of staff already know the context; and the amount of secondary information that has already been collected.

We envisage two extremes of EMMA in practice:
*   *The small single-handed EMMA process*
    EMMA is conducted by an experienced lone EMMA practitioner, with assistance from one or two colleagues with good local knowledge of the crisis-affected area. This takes less time – as little as ten days – but the territory that can be covered is limited.
*   *The large team-based EMMA process*
    EMMA is conducted by a team, led by an experienced EMMA leader who is responsible for training a small team of local interviewers / assessors. This takes longer – four weeks is realistic – but potentially can cover a lot more territory (depending on the size of the team).

The chart in Box 0.14 presents an indicative timetable for these two processes.

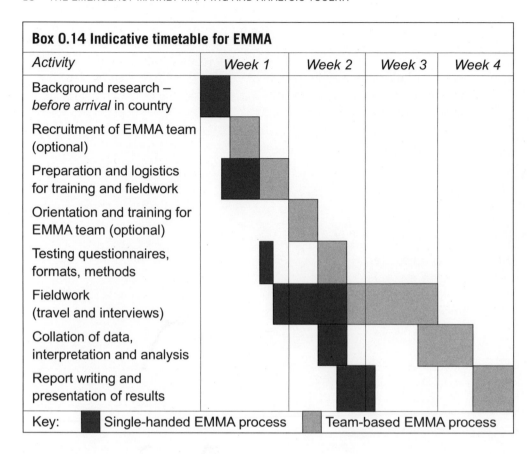

Box 0.14 Indicative timetable for EMMA

Activity	Week 1	Week 2	Week 3	Week 4
Background research – *before arrival* in country				
Recruitment of EMMA team (optional)				
Preparation and logistics for training and fieldwork				
Orientation and training for EMMA team (optional)				
Testing questionnaires, formats, methods				
Fieldwork (travel and interviews)				
Collation of data, interpretation and analysis				
Report writing and presentation of results				

Key: ■ Single-handed EMMA process   ▨ Team-based EMMA process

0.8 Main tools used in EMMA

This section provides a quick introduction (with examples) to the four main tools used in EMMA.

- *Household income and expenditure profiles* – charts illustrating the main sources of income and expenditure
- *Seasonal calendars* – summarizing important seasonal changes in markets and people's lives
- *Market maps* – graphical representations of market systems (before and after emergency onset)
- *Response frameworks* – tables for summarizing emergency-response options and characteristics.

These four tools are used repeatedly throughout EMMA in different steps. The findings from each tool develop in an iterative way: we start with only the roughest approximations, and then revise and refine findings with new information until a 'good-enough' result is achieved (see Box 0.15).

Box 0.15 What are 'good-enough' results?

The amount of time and effort that these tools require depends on context.
*   Detailed household profiles may be unnecessary for a very short-term operation,but invaluable for planning a one- or two-year programme towards economic recovery.
*   Seasonal calendars are more relevant for food security or shelter activities, say, than for the supply of jerry-cans and soap.

The examples in this chapter are final versions, showing a high level of detail.

0.9 Household income and expenditure profiles

Household profiles are a simple way of charting the income and outgoings of a typical target household. This is valuable in order to see:
*   the relative importance of different types of income or expenditure (consumption) (including the food that they produce for themselves);
*   any major changes in income or expenditure caused by the emergency situation.

The profile can be presented as a simple table, or better as a diagram, for example a pie-chart (Box 0.16). Note the approximate percentage figures. An accuracy of plus or minus 5 per cent is good enough for EMMA. Even this is often not possible, or necessary: see 'appropriate imprecision', in section 0.6 above.

Box 0.16 Household-income profile – example

Average household income (May–July 2007)

Value of food produced for home consumption	$100	35%
Sale of own surplus produce (crops / livestock)	$45	5%
Earnings from small business	$31	10%
Salary or wages	$27	10%
Loans received	$14	5%
Remittances received	$0	0%
Value of charity / relief aid	$26	10%
Sale of assets (e.g. livestock)	$42	15%
Total	*$285*	*100%*

Household income and expenditure profiles are mainly used in the gap-analysis strand in EMMA, as follows:

- In Step 1 (essential preparation), profiles may help you to decide if and how the target population can be usefully divided into livelihood groups – with different priority needs or income strategies.
- In Step 2 (market-system selection), profiles help to determine which market systems are critical.
- In Step 5 (fieldwork activities), profiles can be used to collate and summarize information from household interviews, and so verify or challenge your earlier assumptions.

- In Step 7 (complete gap analysis), final comparisons of profiles (baseline, emergency-affected) provide a convenient way to present findings about the impact of the emergency on people's lives.

Box 0.17 shows an example of a comparison of the baseline and emergency-affected expenditure profiles for a group of rural households. Faced with lower income and a drastic reduction in food from their own gardens, they are increasing their food purchases and cutting back on inputs for the next season's food crop, as well as medical and household costs. It is vital to consider the gender dimension to these impacts: who provides the income or work, whose consumption or expenditure is being cut?

Box 0.17 Comparing expenditure profiles 'before' and 'after'

Typical household expenditure	Baseline situation		Emergency-affected	
Value of own-grown food consumed	$100	35%	$13	10%
Food purchased	$12	5%	$44	40%
Fuel (cooking, heat, light)	$27	10%	$21	20%
Other household items	$18	5%	$2	0%
Health / medical	$31	10%	$2	0%
Farm / livestock inputs	$54	20%	$10	10%
Travel / transport	$17	5%	$0	0%
Housing (rent, maintenance)	$26	10%	$22	20%
Total	$285	100%	$114	100%

Baseline situation – $285

Emergency-affected situation – $114

Household profiles and gender

It is important that household profiles such as these distinguish, where possible, between the respective economic roles and responsibilities of women and men within households. Do not assume that their relationships with markets or the crisis impact are the same. Where there are strong differences, it may be necessary to draw up separate profiles, instead of treating 'the household' as a single economic entity.

0.10 Seasonal calendars

Seasonal calendars are a simple way to collate and present information about how geographical regions, market systems, and people's lives vary during the year. EMMA users may be familiar with this tool from Household Economy Analysis methods. Information about seasonal factors is essential in order to understand the following factors:

*   how women and men's livelihoods, sources of income, and necessary expenditures change seasonally;
*   how prices of critical goods, and their volumes of production / trade vary normally during a year;
*   vital changes in the local environment – weather, rainfall, road-access – that are likely to affect the feasibility of different emergency responses.

Seasonal factors are obviously strong in agricultural market systems. We find major seasonal shifts in demand for labour; in weather-related risks such as pests and diseases; and in the supply of produce after harvesting. However, seasonality is not confined to rural livelihoods: for example, the timing of reconstruction work and employment in some industrial sectors and tourism are often seasonally determined.

Seasonal calendars are used in all three EMMA strands: people, markets, and emergency response. In all cases it is best that calendars start from the current date (e.g. September in the examples).

Calendar for emergency-affected economic area

This general calendar for an area can help to indicate which market systems are likely to be most critical at this point in the year (see Box 0.18). This is useful in Steps 1 and 2 (for targeting and market-system selection).

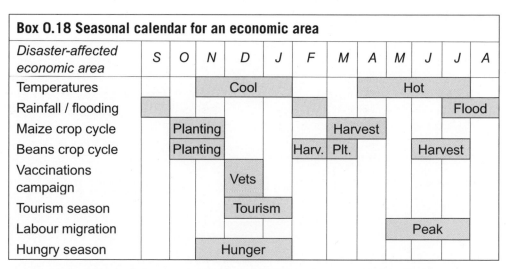

Box 0.18 Seasonal calendar for an economic area

Disaster-affected economic area	S	O	N	D	J	F	M	A	M	J	J	A
Temperatures			Cool					Hot				
Rainfall / flooding											Flood	
Maize crop cycle		Planting					Harvest					
Beans crop cycle		Planting			Harv.	Plt.			Harvest			
Vaccinations campaign				Vets								
Tourism season				Tourism								
Labour migration									Peak			
Hungry season			Hunger									

Interpretation: This example illustrates the importance of the approaching planting season for the main staple crops in this region, and the impending 'hungry season', when food security is a concern.

Household-level calendar for target group

This type of calendar shown in Box 0.19 can be used to collate and summarize information about seasonal factors from household interviews. This helps to identify priority activities and risk factors. This is valuable in Steps 5 and 7 (for fieldwork activities and gap analysis).

Box 0.19 Seasonal calendar for a target group

Target group	S	O	N	D	J	F	M	A	M	J	J	A
Income levels			Low				High					
Loan repayments				$		$				$		
Holiday / festivities				$					$			
School terms		Term A							Term B			
Fodder availability									Low			
Livestock moves		Low ground					High ground					
Casual employment		$					$					
Shelter activities				Brick making				Thatch				

Interpretation: This example highlights opportunities for casual employment that target households normally exploit in October / November in order to prepare for the hungry season, when income levels are low.

Market-system calendar

The type of calendar shown in Box 0.20 provides a convenient way to present findings about seasonal factors in each critical market system. This is useful in Steps 3, 6, and 8 (for preliminary analysis, market mapping, and final analysis).

Box 0.20 Seasonal calendar for a market system												
Market-system (e.g. beans)	S	O	N	D	J	F	M	A	M	J	J	A
Volume of trade			Low			High				Low	High	
Prices at market				Peak $			Low $				Low $	
Input purchases			$				$					
Road conditions	Floods											
Risk of crop pests			High						High			

Interpretation: This example shows how trade volumes (for beans) are normally expected to drop off during October– December, leading to higher prices around New Year. It also illustrates the importance of making inputs available for next season's crops during this period.

0.11 Market-system maps

EMMA revolves around the core concept of the 'market system'. This means the complex web of people, businesses, structures, trends, norms, and rules that determine how any product or service is accessed, produced, exchanged, and made available to different people.

The market-map tool in EMMA is derived from a participatory approach to pro-poor market development in non-emergency contexts, designed by the international NGO Practical Action (Albu and Griffith, 2005). It emphasizes simple and visually engaging methods of communicating and sharing knowledge about complex systems among non-specialists.

Market maps are a powerful way to
- collate and represent information about market systems;
- facilitate discussion, interpretation, and analysis of data within the EMMA team;
- communicate findings about market systems to others.

They are used throughout the market-system analysis strand. EMMA starts with rough, approximate sketches of the market system in Step 3. Then gradually, with more information from interviews and informants in Step 5, EMMA builds on and revises these maps until a final 'good-enough' version is achieved in Step 6.

There are three sections to the market map – as illustrated by the examples in Boxes 0.7 and 0.21.

1. *The market chain*
    The centre portion of the map shows the supply chain (also known as the value chain) of different market actors who buy and sell the product as it moves from primary producers / suppliers to the final consumers / buyers. These actors include, for example, small-holder farmers, larger-scale producers, traders, processors, transporters, wholesalers, retailers, and of course consumers.
2. *Key infrastructure and support services*
    Below the market chain, the map shows various types of critical infrastructure, inputs, and services that are provided by other service enterprises, organizations, and governments. These actors and services are those which support the market system's overall functioning or performance, even though they do not directly buy or sell the item.
3. *The market environment*
    Above the market chain, the map shows other factors that strongly influence how producers, traders, consumers, and other market actors operate in the emergency situation. These factors include formal policies, regulations, and rules; informal social norms – such as gender roles, official and business practices; trends and current affairs – including patterns of social and political conflict, and economic and environmental trends.

Market maps are used in EMMA – in particular – to show the changes (impact) created in the market system by the emergency situation. This is illustrated by the second map of Haitian Beans market: Box 0.21. In this example, the map of the emergency-affected situation is used to highlight critical issues, and areas of partial or complete disruption to market actors, linkages, or services in the market system. For example:

*   Obstruction of rural roads and bridges by landslides has severely impacted on district-level traders.
*   Women garden producers have lost their crops, so their households are dependent on purchased food at a time when they would normally be selling small food surpluses to village traders.
*   Food aid is reaching some landless rural households, by-passing the normal supply chain.

Market maps can also be used (in Step 8) to capture and analyse market information. In Box 0.22, information about the number of market actors and the total estimated volumes of trade has been over-laid on to the earlier market map.

This type of data mapping can reveal bottlenecks in supply chains, tell EMMA about the market system's capacity to meet priority needs, indicate where local procurement is possible, or even highlight opportunities for other non-conventional emergency responses (see Step 8 and 9).

Box 0.21 Emergency-affected market map – 'beans' example from Haiti

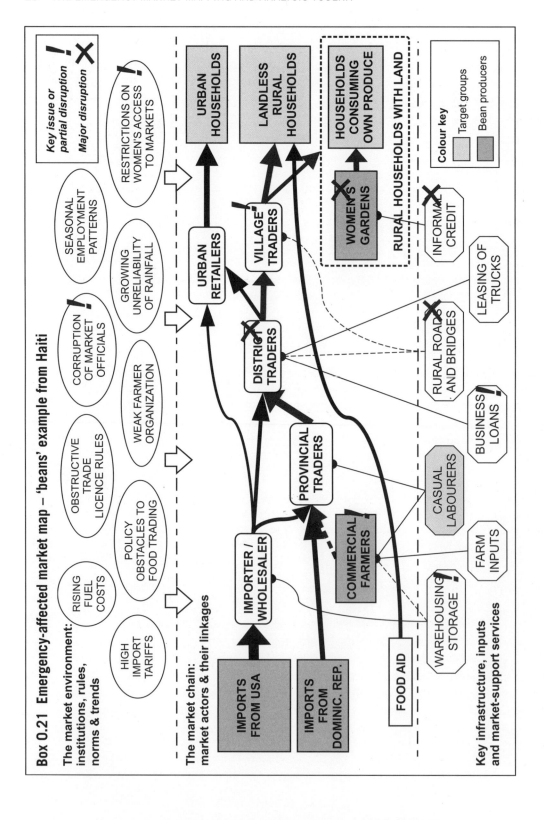

Box 0.22 Market-system map overlaid with trade-volume data

The market chain:
market actors & their linkages

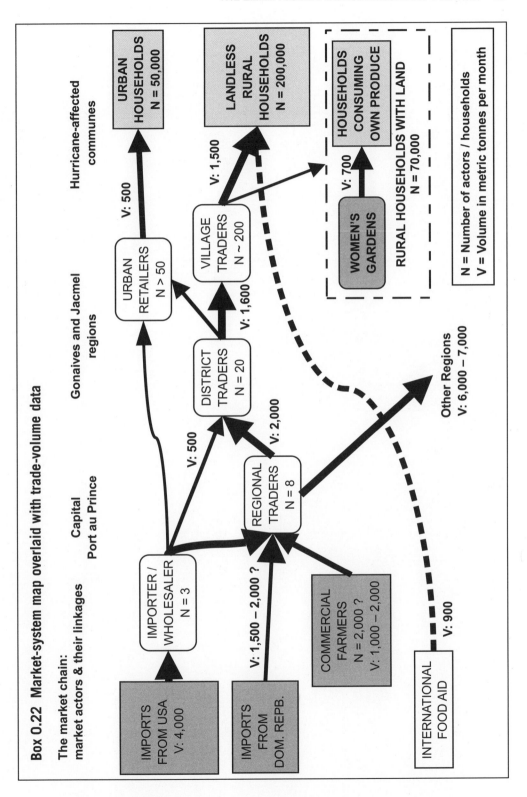

0.12 Emergency-response frameworks

EMMA employs two forms of response framework:

*   *Response Options Framework* (Step 9) to summarize information about the full range of plausible response options emerging from the EMMA fieldwork and analysis;
*   *Response Recommendations Framework* (Step 10) to present to decision makers a small number of the most feasible response recommendations.

These frameworks tools are useful (like LogFrames) for systematically thinking through and rationalizing recommendations; and presenting results concisely and logically to EMMA's decision-making audience.

The illustrative examples in Boxes 0.23 and 0.24 are a partial extract from an EMMA study of the wood-fuel market system in and around large camps for displaced people in Pakistan.

The first framework (Box 0.23) provides decision makers with an essential summary of the EMMA findings. This enables clear explanation of the rationale for the recommended responses. These can then be presented in a second table (Box 0.24), which summarizes the key risks and assumptions and timing issues related to each proposal.

It can also be used to summarize the likely effect on target groups and market systems which EMMA envisages; along with indicators of change that should be monitored.

Box 0.23 Response-options framework – example

Response option	Feasi-bility	Advantages	Disadvantages	Timing
1. Distribution of spare (confiscated) supplies from Forest Dept.	Low	Would have immediate economic and environmental impacts. Would utilize existing/ useless stocks; in the short term, would slow deforestation; simple distribution programme.	Requires warehouses, distribution staff. Limits integration with market in town and camp. Wood may be sold on, as people are now coping by scavenging. Legal obstacles in transporting wood through district borders? Need to determine market rate for purchase and quantity.	2–3 weeks
2. Distribution involving camp-based retailers and vouchers	Med-ium	Inject cash into camp economy, thus creating many secondary beneficiaries; would create more local vendors.	Very few camp retailers with any capacity; no storage or infrastructure inside camps; open to fraud. Start-up slow – with procurement and beneficiary identification process.	2 months to implement
3. Promotion of fuel-saving (efficiency) techniques	High	Transferrable skills, creating savings for women at household level. Addresses child protection. Good for environment. Clear exit strategy. Easily integrated with other programmes e.g. pressure cookers	Requires intense inputs from community development/mobilizers. Requires lots of training and materials. Time of women. Risky because it requires behaviour change over a long time. Hard to monitor impact.	Behavioural change, the longer the better
4. Refilling of gas canisters; conditional on school attendance	High	Less firewood usage, time-saving. Incentives for sending children to school. Reduces protection issues. Clear exit strategy: reduces distributions.	Gas is twice the price of firewood; risky using inside tents; IDPs cannot afford refilling on own. May increase dependency on aid; makes school attendance linked to reward, instead of intrinsic worth; not sustainable.	Can be started soon
5. Cash distribution	Low	Injects money into the camp economy. Positive effect on household economies but no effect on firewood market; gives households choices.	Potential for inflation; corruption; no exit strategy; no way to ensure that cash is used for firewood; people might continue to send children for firewood collection instead of buying it.	Quick response

Box 0.24 Response-recommendations matrix – example

Response activities or combinations	Key risks and assumptions	Timing issues	Likely effect on market system and target groups	Indicators
Fuel-efficient stoves and cooking techniques • Stove distribution • Cooking techniques • Sensitization on fuel efficiency, forestation, child-protection issues	We have access to camps. Women have time, are willing to learn and use stoves properly. We can find trained staff.	1–2 months to make an impact	• Reduce household firewood expenses. • Increase fuel efficiency at household level. • Small – but important – positive effect on environment. • Improved protection (fewer kids collecting wood).	# of stoves distributed and used by IDPs. Comparison of wood-fuel consumption old vs new.
Fuel for school attendance • Combination of gas-canister refilling and incentives for school attendance. • Sensitization on fuel efficiency, forestation, child-protection issues.	IDPs are willing to send children to school. IDPs practise safe cooking techniques.	2–3 weeks	• Reduce amount of household income spent on fuel. • Students' attendance increases.	% increase in complete attendance. % decrease in amount of household income spent on fuel

PART TWO
EMMA TOOLKIT

STEP 1
Essential preparation

Photo credit: Howard Davies

Displaced women from Thampattai camp, Sri Lanka, planning activities following the tsunami

Step 1 covers the essential activities that are needed in order to prepare for an EMMA investigation. These activities can begin before EMMA teams arrive in the emergency zone and before terms of reference for the analysis have been agreed. They include preparation and briefings in-country, while the practical arrangements for the EMMA process are put in place. Crucially, they include the clear identification of the target population for assistance – disaggregated into different groups where possible to reflect diverse needs.

Before starting Step 1, the EMMA leader should

o   be closely familiar with all the steps in the EMMA toolkit.

1.1 Overview of Step 1

Objectives

- Obtain a good-enough initial understanding of the general emergency situation.
- Organize the EMMA team, their work-space, logistics, and essential support.
- Establish clear terms of reference for the EMMA exercise with management
- Agree who the intended target population are, and where they are located.

Activities

Section 1.2: Background research (before arrival)
- Review any pre-crisis livelihoods assessments.
- Review general economic analyses, information about disaster area.
- Review any recent damage / impact assessments.

Section 1.3: Consultations with colleagues (in-country or in the disaster area)
- Review latest emergency needs assessments.
- Clarify geographical and / or sectoral mandate of agency.
- Clarify the agency's response time-frame.
- Arrange briefings on political and security considerations.

Section 1.4: Setting up an EMMA working base
- Establish work-space (meetings, training, group work).
- Confirm the EMMA team membership, roles, and responsibilities.
- Organize fieldwork logistics, travel, and accommodation plans.

Sections 1.5 and 1.6: Population targeting and disaggregation
- Identify who the target population are.
- Draft a general seasonal calendar for their local economy.
- Define distinct target groups within the target population, including by livelihood strategy, wealth or social status, culture or ethnicity, and gender.

Timing

This step requires consultation with, and co-operation from, colleagues and other agencies. The time needed depends on the scale of the disaster area, on the level of administrative support available in the emergency zone, and the urgency of programming deadlines. EMMA teams who are familiar with the emergency-affected area and local agency operations may complete this step in as little as two days. However, in other circumstances these activities can easily take up most of the first week of the EMMA assignment.

Key outputs

- EMMA terms of reference agreed with country management (preferably in writing).
- Summary information about the target population (see Boxes 1.5 and 1.8).

1.2 Background research

Background research begins before arrival in the emergency-affected area. A day or two on the internet before departure can be very rewarding; and may provide useful material to read on the journey.

The main aims of background research are...

* to become familiar with any impact assessments, or needs assessments, that have already been produced by agencies on the ground;
* to identify any general economic analyses and other background information about the area, including maps and basic statistics (e.g. about population, food security, culture etc.);
* to locate any existing reports that describe the 'normal' livelihood strategies or seasonal calendars of the emergency-affected population, including cultural considerations;
* to establish useful contacts in the country – potential key informants.

Box 1.1 Useful websites for rapid background research

RELIEF-WEB: for general news and updates on emergency situation (organized by countries and sectors), lots of maps, OCHA Situation Reports, Cluster Reports
www.reliefweb.int

FEWS-NET: for food-security information, descriptions of livelihood zones and market profiles, data on markets and trade, food security, maps of trade flows
www.fews.net

MAP-ACTION: source of maps and technical information, for example on trade flow
www.mapaction.org

UN OCHA: 'Who Does What Where' – a contact-management directory
http://3w.unocha.org

LOG-CLUSTER: logistics information relevant to conducting fieldwork, road conditions and travel times, maps and supplier databases (for contacts)
www.logcluster.org

UNICEF: for general country-overview information, especially re water and sanitation, health sector, essential household items. Focus on children's needs
www.unicef.org

WFP: for information on food-security issues, search by country, CFSVA and CFSAM reports
www.wfp.org

UNHCR: usually good for information on shelter needs, especially re refugee and IDP movements
www.unhcr.org

IOM: International Office for Migration – reports relating to movement of people and shelter needs
www.iom.org

IFRC: for links to national Red Cross organizations (especially relevant after natural disasters)
www.ifrc.org

Box 1.2 Useful websites for detailed research

FAO and FAOSTAT: for reports and data on food production, food security, and balance sheets
www.fao.org / http://faostat.fao.org

WFP VAM: the Vulnerability Analysis and Mapping branch, for detailed reports about food insecurity
http://www.wfp.org/food-security

Microfinance Gateway: for country profiles on micro-finance institutions and credit services
www.microfinancegateway.com

Food Economy Group: resource for Household Economy Analysis (HEA) reports and guidance
www.feg-consulting.com

Livelihoods Connect: resource for Sustainable Livelihoods approach, reports, and guidance
www.eldis.org/go/topics/dossiers/livelihoods-connect

SEEP-Network: good for web-links to country-specific sites on micro-finance, enterprise development
www.seepnetwork.org

BDS-Knowledge: huge library of reports on enterprise development, market analyses
www.bdsknowledge.org

UNDP: for more detailed reports on long-term development policies and livelihood strategies
www.undp.org

VALUE CHAIN DEVELOPMENT WIKI: good practice in value-chain development
http://apps.develebridge.net/amap/index.php/Value_Chain_Development

MICRO-LINKS: Micro-enterprise development in conflict-affected environments; project site and resources
www.microlinks.org/ev_en.php?ID=19747_201&ID2=DO_TOPIC

1.3. Consultations with colleagues

Upon arrival at the in-country office or making contact with the emergency focal point, EMMA practitioners need to establish relationships with the staff on the ground. It is essential to establish a clear TOR that defines the scope of work. The EMMA team must be briefed on its roles and responsibilities.

EMMA orientation for managers (and donors)

EMMA is still a new approach. It is important to brief managers (and quite possibly donors too) about what the EMMA process aims to achieve. The introductory chapter provides useful materials for these conversations.

Good talking points may include the following:

* Markets may offer a fast, effective, empowering way to respond to priority needs.
* Market recovery is a necessary aspect of livelihood rehabilitation and food security.
* Inappropriate humanitarian responses can do major further damage to livelihoods
* Women and men use markets in different ways, and are affected differently by crisis.
* Market actors' 'behaviour' can indicate whether responses are working as intended.
* Crises in market systems can also be opportunities for improvement and reform.

Find out what management issues the EMMA approach may raise. How open-minded are decision-makers to unconventional or indirect interventions? For example, are there donor restrictions on the types of humanitarian response that they will fund? Is it feasible to think of support to market actors (e.g. assistance to traders) in a critical market system?

Understand the agency's mandate and capabilities

Every humanitarian agency has its own specialisms, capabilities, and planning time-frames, which help to determine the scope of its feasible response options.

* Find out what geographical mandate the agency is taking on – what area it is likely to cover; what languages it works in.
* Understand the agency's sectoral specialisms (shelter, child protection, gender, water and sanitation, etc.), the agency's skill sets, and its resources (staff numbers, vehicles).
* Confirm what time-frame the agency is planning for. Do managers want EMMA to help to inform the operational activities for the next three months, six months, a year, or longer?
* Get briefed on the agency's pre-crisis operations in-country, if any. Does the agency have objectives for long-term development work, i.e. an interest in transitional programming?

Emergency briefing for EMMA team

Arrange for front-line staff, field-based managers, and sector specialists (e.g. shelter, wat/san, food security) to brief you. This may be easier if it is done jointly.

- Find out the latest information on damage. Get hold of any emergency needs assessments. Refer to any emergency web forums or www.reliefweb.int for assessments from colleague agencies.
- Find out what is already being done or planned by various humanitarian agencies. For example: check UN OCHA's 'Who Does What Where' matrix at http://3w.unocha.org
- Talk to long-term development staff (internal or external, UNDP) who know the specific region well.
- Join the relevant cluster group or co-ordination meetings. Contact the cluster-group leader as a potential key informant.

Box 1.3 UN cluster groups

Cluster groups or other co-ordination meetings are generally the forums in emergencies for sharing information and avoiding duplication. You may find specialists within the cluster who can offer valuable information and insights (including contacts for key informants), or be willing to participate in EMMA.

Cluster groups may also value EMMA findings directly. After cyclone Yemyin in Pakistan in 2007, the recommended shelter kit for 10,000 displaced households included floor mats which could perhaps have been sourced locally. An EMMA analysis exploring local production capability would have been valuable to the Shelter cluster.

Political or security considerations

EMMA teams need to be sensitive to political and security considerations, both during the EMMA fieldwork and in terms of the response options that EMMA recommends. Make sure you are invited to security briefings.

In conflict situations, especially, remember the following:

- Market systems may be part of the root cause of conflict; for example: due to competition over access to resources.
- Special sensitivities are needed regarding response option; for example: to avoid responses that aggravate conflict, or create perceptions of agency bias
- The most vulnerable and affected groups may not necessarily be the poorest; for example: during the civil unrest in western Kenya in 2008, the worst-affected households were (relatively wealthy) small-holders and businesses targeted for ethnic and political reasons.

Further reading on market analysis and conflict: see material in the EMMA reference manual on CD-ROM, including:

- ODI Humanitarian Practitioners Network: *Food Security and Livelihoods Programming in Conflict* (Jaspars and Maxwell, 2009)
- The SEEP Network: *Market Development in Crisis-affected Environments* (Market Development Working Group, 2007)

- USAID Office of Conflict Management and Mitigation Guide: *Livelihood and Conflict: A Toolkit for Intervention* (CMM, 2005)

Build your contacts

EMMA is all about people and knowledge: find out who is who.

Start building a contact list of colleagues, staff in other agencies, potential key informants, key officials, main traders, and market-actors.

Do not neglect the knowledge of local ancillary staff. Drivers, guards, cooks, and office cleaners often understand from personal experience the impact of an emergency on ordinary households and local markets very well.

1.4. Establish a working base for the EMMA team

EMMA work-space

Set up an EMMA 'base camp': a space where the EMMA team can work, meet, train, and store information. Try to make this a place where calm reflection is possible – quiet enough for the EMMA team to think, discuss, and learn.

Ideally, the EMMA base-camp will have
- a large table and chairs, and wall-space for maps and flip-charts
- a telephone for arranging meetings, computer and internet access.

Confirm the EMMA team membership, roles, and responsibilities

The size of an EMMA team will depend on the scale of the emergency (number of locations), the urgency of the need for results, and the resources available. Experience to date suggests that EMMA works best when two people cover each market system selected (in Step 2) in any district or location. In most contexts, it is essential from a practical perspective, and to meet gender standards, to have both women and men in the team – for interviewing households, for example.

For large team-based EMMA processes in which an experienced EMMA practitioner leads a locally convened team of researchers / assessors (see section 0.7), it will usually be necessary to train and orientate colleagues broadly beforehand in EMMA concepts and methods (see Step 3).

Even in a simple two-handed EMMA process, some aspects of fieldwork (Step 5) – especially information gathering for gap analysis – may benefit from co-opting other field-staff; for example, to conduct interviews with target households. These people may also need orientation in interview methods.

Training guidance for these scenarios is provided in the EMMA reference manual on CD-ROM.

Fieldwork planning: travel, accommodation, logistics

Begin planning for the fieldwork as soon as possible. Talk to logisticians, adminis-trators, and drivers about road conditions and travel times (see www.logcluster. org), or check the updated emergency information at the www.reliefweb.int link.

- Plan for accommodation and vehicles.
- Book meeting rooms or spaces for preparation, training, and analysis work.
- Arrange meetings for consultations with colleagues and other agencies' staff – both before and after the fieldwork phase.
- Find out which are the important market-days of the week in the local area.

1.5. Population targeting

Confirm target population

As early as possible, EMMA teams must confirm who the target population are.

Box 1.4 'Target population' defined

In EMMA, 'target population' means the mass of people who ultimately benefit from the emergency response. These are not necessarily the individuals who are directly involved in the agency's action.

For example, after a cyclone, youths are employed on cash-for-work basis to clear debris from irrigation ditches. They are directly involved; but the ultimate beneficiaries – and hence the 'target population' – are large numbers of small farmers, agricultural workers, and their families whose food security is to be restored.

How to do this

Talk to colleagues and review emergency needs assessments. This will be largely a management decision, based on emergency needs assessments. It will also reflect the agency's geographical or sectoral mandate. Key information that defines the target population includes the following:

- The estimated population numbers: how many people are at risk and/or in need of assistance?
- Their location – approximate geographical area most at risk, approximate distance (or travel time) from major commercial centres or ports. A map is useful at this point.
- Any characteristics that distinguish particular households as a priority target for the agency: who are those that are most in need of assistance or most at risk?

| Box 1.5 Examples of target populations ||||
Target	Numbers	Locations	Agency focus
Flood-affected rural households	70,000 households	South-west delta area (approx 1,500 km²), 6–8 hours from national port	Small-holders and landless families
Earthquake victims	120,000 households	50 villages/towns within 30 km of earthquake epicentre at Khanit	Families with elderly members and vulnerable children
Internally displaced families	30,000 households	Four IDP camps in the Shalinha valley, 3 hours from provincial capital	All displaced people within camps

1. Essential preparation

Basic livelihood information

The use of a livelihoods approach in emergency assessments is increasingly common (Young et al., 2001). EMMA requires at the very least some essential information about the livelihood strategies of the target population. As more details are understood, EMMA teams will then divide the target population into separate groups according to differential needs (section 1.6).

However, these preliminary questions should set the scene to begin with.

*   What were their main sources of employment, income or other important livelihood activities?
*   What types of land or other natural resource did / do they depend on?
*   What are the seasonal patterns of their lives and key activities at this time of year?
*   Were there any major risks to people's livelihoods that existed before the current crisis?
*   What are the typical coping strategies being adopted by affected households following the shock?

How to do this

For detailed guidance on livelihoods concepts and methods, see the EMMA reference manual on CD-ROM.

EMMA assumes that there is not usually time to survey the target population directly at this point. Therefore, you must rely on secondary reports and general knowledge of colleagues. Critical assumptions can be checked later during gap-analysis fieldwork (Step 5).

- Review the emergency needs assessments / damage reports for clues.
- Look for livelihood-assessment reports coming from long-term development programmes.
- Talk to colleagues and staff who know the area or the population well.
- Find or draft a rough seasonal calendar for the area.

1.6 Disaggregation of target groups

Do not assume that all affected households have similar needs, opportunities, and vulnerabilities. As far as possible, the different experiences, capabilities, and needs of women and men, and the differences between other social, ethnic, or age-based groups, should be taken into account. The choice of critical market systems, the results of gap analysis, and hence the final response recommendations may well vary from group to group.

There are often huge differences between what women and men need from markets, and the ways in which they access and use market systems. The IASC Gender Handbook includes a useful section on gender and livelihoods in emergencies (Inter-Agency Standing Committee, 2006, pp. 83–88). The same is true of different age groups and sometimes of different cultural or ethnic groups. EMMA teams need to decide which criteria (Box 1.6) to use for disaggregating target groups pragmatically, taking into account their agency mandate.

Box 1.6 Criteria for defining different target groups

Livelihood strategies

What are the most useful socio-economic categories of the population? Different groups may have substantially different sources of income, ways of making a living and engaging with markets, even in the same location: e.g. farmers, fishermen, casual labourers.

Relative wealth

Differences in relative wealth, social status, and assets are often important factors in determining how emergencies affect households, and they make a big difference in how particular households access and use market systems.

Gender roles

Gender roles and culture influence how women and men access and use markets, along with other factors such as land, natural resources, and other assets. Food crops are often the responsibility of women, whereas men control use of cash crops. These factors affect vulnerability to crisis and the strategies that people use to cope with disasters.

Age, social, cultural, and ethnic exclusion

Age, culture, social divisions, and ethnic divisions all influence how people access and use markets. These factors are especially important to consider if they played a role in triggering the emergency (e.g. in conflict situations).

Number of target groups

Remember that the needs of each group will need to be investigated separately, which will add time to the fieldwork and complexity to the EMMA analysis. Strictly, every target group requires its own separate household survey – in Step 5. In practice, EMMA teams can usually afford only to distinguish between at most two or three different target groups.

The summary results of disaggregating the target population will look something like Box 1.7.

Box 1.7 Target groups – examples		
Target group	*Households*	*Locations etc.*
Displaced farming households in camps	7,000	Jezila (3,000); Matran (4,000)
Casual labourers (fishery sector)	3,000	In 14 villages around Ghela
Households with extra-vulnerable individuals, and female-headed	500	Distributed throughout area
Total target population	*10,500*	

How to do this

Agencies tend to have different emphases and priorities which influence how they define target groups. Some agencies focus on productive groups, some on household types, age differences or gender differences, some on geographical locations or ethnic distinctions.

It is a good idea to adopt categories that are familiar to colleagues. For example:
- differences in their livelihoods strategies (sources of income) before the crisis;
- differences in their relative wealth within the wider community;
- differences in their current location / situation; or
- differences in other vulnerability factors, especially ethnicity or gender.

Information about the target population's characteristics and needs will often still be sketchy at this stage. However, EMMA assumes that you will not usually have time or resources to conduct a detailed survey of the target population. Therefore, EMMA teams must decide – pragmatically – what level of grouping is feasible and has operational value in their circumstances.

Box 1.8 A seasonal calendar for target population

At this early stage of EMMA before selecting critical markets, it is useful to begin sketching out a seasonal calendar for the target groups and their local economic area. This will be used in Step 2. Remember that women and men often have very different seasonal roles and responsibilities.

Seasonal calendars may be found during background research (section 1.2). FAO is a good source, especially for crop calendars. Look out for household economic analysis (HEA) studies also. FEWS NET publish calendars too.

If not, a 'good-enough' seasonal calendar may be constructed from brief discussions with colleagues and local staff who understand people's livelihoods and the local economy.

The level of detail needed at this stage is low: a brief explanation of how and why groups are defined separately. As Box 1.8 describes, you must rely on secondary reports and general knowledge of colleagues or key informants in other agencies. Critical assumptions can be checked later during gap-analysis fieldwork (Step 5).

Checklist for Step 1

o   Do background research, using websites and secondary reports.

o   On arrival, attend security briefings. Organize logistics and administrative support. Establish contacts.

o   Attend orientation meeting with country-programme management. Agree terms of reference.

o   Review emergency needs assessments and damage reports.

o   Confirm details of the target population and identify any important target groups or characteristics that divide the target population.

o   Establish an EMMA base-camp; organize EMMA team.

o   Begin logistics arrangements (vehicle, accommodation) for fieldwork.

o   Get briefings from field-based managers and sector specialists.

o   Set up future meetings with key informants, donors, and other agencies – e.g. cluster group.

STEP 2
Market selection

Photo credit: Toby Adamson/Oxfam

A truck being loaded at a market, Haiti

Step 2 involves selecting the specific market systems that are the highest priorities for EMMA investigation, from a humanitarian perspective. Although different markets (for example, markets for rice and fertilizer) often interact, every traded item or service has its own unique market system. For practical reasons, EMMA analyses each critical market system separately as far as possible. Since time, information, and resources for EMMA are limited, careful selection is vital. This depends on various different operational and humanitarian criteria.

Before starting Step 2, the EMMA leader should have...

o   developed a 'good-enough' general understanding of the emergency situation;

o   organized the EMMA team, a work space, and necessary support;

o   agreed clear terms of reference for the EMMA exercise with management;

o   agreed who and where the intended target population (ultimate beneficiaries) are.

2.1 Overview of Step 2

Objectives

- Select which *critical market systems* will be the subject of EMMA investigation.
- Outline the *key analytical questions* that need answering for each of these systems.

Activities

Sections 2.2 and 2.3: Select critical market systems
- Review the priority needs of the target population's different groups: e.g. food, essential household items, shelter.
- Consider other needs related to livelihoods, assets, and incomes.
- Select critical market systems for EMMA.

Section 2.4: Identify key analytical questions
- Consult with colleagues, cluster-group members, key informants.
- Identify the key analytical questions for each selected market system.

Key outputs

- Final selection / short list of critical market systems for EMMA to study
- Clear rationale for the selection
- List of key analytical questions in each critical market system

---

Box 2.1 'Critical market systems' and 'key analytical questions' defined

Critical market systems
In an emergency situation, 'critical' market systems are those that played, play, or could play a major role in ensuring survival, and/or protecting livelihoods of the target population.

Key analytical questions
Market systems are usually selected because agency staff have specific ideas or expectations about the operational value that EMMA will add. 'Key analytical questions' frame these ideas, and thus help teams to keep them in mind throughout the EMMA process.

2.2 Brainstorming options for market-system selection

Once the target population is reasonably well defined (see section 1.6), the selection of market systems for investigation using EMMA must take place. Every crop, non-food item, or service has its own particular market system. This means that it is necessary to decide pragmatically which market systems - i.e. which items, crops, products

– are most critical for EMMA investigation. This can never be a perfect decision, since it is very unlikely that you will have as much information as you would like. Selection is best done in two stages:
1. *Brainstorming:* broadening out ideas to generate lots of options.
2. *Filtering:* narrowing the options, using criteria of feasibility, timing, agency mandate, security.

The first task is to draw up a long list of candidates for inclusion as critical market systems. This list should reflect the target population's priority needs, their pre-crisis economic activities, and their current options for restoring income and food security.

The brainstorming task is more effective if EMMA teams can think outside the conventional humanitarian box. The three categories of market system in Box 2.2 are useful to think about.

Box 2.2 Three categories of 'critical' market system		
For ensuring survival	*For protecting and promoting livelihoods*	
(Supply) market systems that provide food, essential household items, or services to meet urgent survival needs	(Supply) market systems that provide essential tools, replace assets, provide agricultural inputs, or deliver vital services	(Income) market systems that provide jobs, create demand for wage labour, or provide buyers for target groups' own produce
Examples: Staple food items, clothing and blankets, shelter materials, essential household items, soap, buckets, bedding, tents, fuel or firewood	*Examples:* Agricultural tools, fertilizer, fodder, seeds, pumps, veterinary services, credit services, fishing nets, boats, transport services	*Examples:* Cash crops, livestock, fish and forest products, agricultural and casual labour, re-construction activities, other employment industries

Do not assume that critical market systems must mainly be those that relate to survival needs.

Market systems which supply productive assets and inputs may be good candidates for EMMA. So too are market systems which provide a direct source of urgently needed income: getting their crops or livestock to market, or restoring access to paid employment, is often a very high priority for affected populations.

Box 2.3 EMMA goes beyond survival needs
After Cyclone Nargis in Myanmar in 2008, many rice-farming households in the Ayeyarwady delta said that obtaining seeds and tools in time to plant their next crop was a more urgent need than restoring their homes (e.g. to Sphere shelter standards).

Where do market systems begin and end?

There is sometimes no easy way to define the boundaries of a market system for analysis. All market systems interact with others: for example, staple cereal markets interact with labour markets, fertilizer markets, and transport markets. It may not make sense to independently analyse market systems that actually supply key services for others, or substituted goods, or complementary services.

Given limited time and resources, it is essential to make a quick and pragmatic decision about where to draw a boundary around the system: including as many relevant factors as possible, but still keeping the analysis task manageable. For example, if you think transport services are critical only for their role in sorghum trading, it would be sensible to consider transport as a support service within the sorghum market system. But if transport services play many different important roles in people's livelihoods, it might be worth the time to analyse transport services as a whole market system in its own right.

Diverse needs of different target groups

It is vital that the list of market systems takes into account the diverse needs of the different target groups within the population that were identified in section 1.6.

Box 2.4 Selecting critical markets and identifying needs are not the same thing

There is a difference between identifying 'needs' and selecting 'market systems', especially in economic activities. Consider the following, for example.

*   *A poor coastal community who live by fishing for the local tourist hotel market:* iftheir main emergency problem is a loss of boats and nets, then EMMA needs to concentrate on understanding the market system for fishing inputs. However, if they lack buyers for their catch, then EMMA needs to examine the whole market system for fish from fisher-folk through to consumers in hotels or the city.
*   *Landless households who mainly depend on seasonal agricultural work:* if their main employers are local large-scale export-orientated wheat farmers, then the critical EMMA priority may be the national market system for wheat.

How to do this

*   Look at recent rapid or emergency needs assessments, and security updates.

*   Review previous studies of people's livelihoods and the local economy (ref. Step 1), i.e. what is known about the sources of food and income for different target groups.

- Consult as broadly as possible with local colleagues who have already visited the disaster area, or who know the population well.

Even without background research, it is often possible to get a 'good-enough' picture of target groups' livelihood strategies by talking to local staff, for example development-project officers. Do not overlook people such as drivers, secretaries, and office cleaners, who may understand the lives of ordinary people very well.

The results of 'brainstorming' might look like Box 2.5.

Box 2.5 Long-list of market-system options (example)		
re Survival needs	re Livelihood needs	re Sources of income
Target group A (rural households with small-holdings)		
• Maize (staple food) • Beans (staple food) • Plastic sheets (roofing)	• Agriculture inputs (seeds and fertilizer)	• Beans (sales of own beans surplus) • Fishery sector (wages for casual work)
Target group B (landless and displaced households)		
• Maize (staple food) • Beans (staple food) • Blankets	• Transport services to city (for seasonal casual work)	• Fishery sector (wages for casual work) • Financial services (remittances from relatives)

Box 2.6 Selecting alternative income markets for refugees

In some crisis situations – especially those involving refugees and displaced populations – people need to find completely new and alternative sources of income to replace livelihoods that are no longer possible: for example, former farming households deprived of access to land.

In these circumstances, EMMA cannot use previous income strategies as a guide to selecting which income market systems to study. Instead selection needs a more thorough understanding of the local economy: where opportunities for new income and employment may exist. It must be sensitive to local political considerations, and to the target population's relationship with the host community.

Market-system selection in these situations is much more complex – needing more time and care – than the rough-and-ready process described in this section. Businesses, employers, local NGOs, micro-finance institutions, and other key informants on economic opportunities should be consulted. See the EMMA reference manual on CD-ROM for further suggestions.

2.3 Selecting critical market systems

The next task is to narrow the long-list down to a manageable short-list of EMMA candidates.

In some emergency situations there will already be a strong consensus about this, based on emergency needs assessment, or simply on people's gut reaction to the crisis. However, it is worth doing the selection systematically, using clear criteria, as shown in Box 2.7, for example.

Box 2.7 Criteria for selecting market systems

- Which market systems are *most significant or urgent* for protecting the life and livelihoods of women and men?
- What are *government agencies or other large agencies* doing, or planning to do?
- Which market systems have been *most affected by the emergency*?
- Which market systems *fit the agency's sectoral mandate and competencies* well?
- What are the critical issues in terms of *response timing or seasonality*?
- Which market systems appear to have scope for *feasible response options*?

Remember that response decisions will be made with or without EMMA. EMMA aims to influence these decisions. To do this, you will need to demonstrate clearly and communicate effectively the evidenced-based reasons behind the response options proposed.

Criterion 1: Most significant or urgently relevant market systems

Some market systems are more important to women's and men's survival or livelihoods than others. It should be possible to eliminate some candidate systems simply because they serve only non-urgent needs, e.g. replacement of assets that can wait until a later recovery phase; or because they have only marginal importance e.g. they were a source of income that was small before the emergency.

If EMMA already has a sketch of target households' income and expenditure profiles (see section 0.9), this can help – by indicating which income sources or expenditures were major or minor. Remember to consider gender differences here: whose income and whose expenditure is involved? If there are good reasons to prioritize women's economic activities, for example, this should influence the assessment.

Criterion 2: Most-affected market systems

Sometimes market systems are relatively unaffected by an emergency situation. EMMA selection can ignore even important market systems if there are good indications that they are still operating well: i.e. with trade continuing and the target population's needs being met.

Criterion 3: Agency / donor mandate and competencies

There is little point in conducting EMMA in a market system if it is known in advance that the recommendations arising from the analysis are unlikely to be implemented.

- Many agencies have pre-established mandates: for example, to focus on the needs of children, women, or the elderly. Also each has its specific area of competency, with a focus on a particular emergency sector: food security, shelter, livelihoods recovery, water and sanitation, etc.
- Donors also often have their own preferences for the kinds of response that they would like to fund.
- Governments may have political reasons for encouraging or discouraging certain kinds of response.

These sorts of factor need to be included – pragmatically and openly – as criteria in the selection of critical market systems. The needs, economic activities, and responsibilities of vulnerable groups (women, elderly, minorities) should carry appropriate weight in the assessment.

Criterion 4: Seasonality and timing

Seasonality factors can play a major role in helping to select which market systems are critical.

- The importance to people of many market systems (especially agricultural) varies according to the time of year.
- Some emergency responses are more or less feasible, depending on the season.

The general seasonal calendar that you sketched in section 1.6 draws attention to these issues.

2.
Market
selection

> ### Box 2.8 Seasonal factors in selection – some examples
>
> After Cyclone Nargis in Myanmar in 2008, many farmers were concerned about planting next season's paddy crop. In deciding whether to analyse markets for rice seed and agricultural tools, it was critical to know whether or not agricultural 'deadlines' could be met.
>
> Also after Cyclone Nargis, shelter reconstruction was a very visible priority need. However, durable roofing materials (mainly thatch) were available during two seasons of the year only – and this dictated when the emergency response could happen.
>
> After the Asian tsunami in 2004, some agencies rushed into cash-for-work programmes without realizing that their response timing clashed with the planting season for annual crops. This unnecessarily increased food insecurity later.
>
> After the civil unrest in Kenya in 2008, many agencies focused on shelter programmes for displaced people. However, many of those displaced were more worried about obtaining replacement seeds and fertilizer, and using them before the rainy season started.

Criterion 5: The plans of government and other agencies

The existing or planned activities of governments and other humanitarian agencies are key factors to consider. Large-scale programmes – planned food distributions, for example – can have a major impact, either directly on the 'gaps' faced by target groups (see Step 7) and/or indirectly through their impact on the relevant market systems (Step 8).

If other agencies' programmes look like being important factors in the EMMA analysis, it is a good idea to consult and if possible involve them in the EMMA selection process.

Even when a target population's needs are already being met by humanitarian actions (for example through food distributions), it may still be valuable to analyse that market system. EMMA can contribute to the analysis of when or how an existing programme can be phased out.

Criterion 6: Emergency-response feasibility

Even at this early stage, EMMA participants in market-system selection sometimes already have some strong views about what kinds of emergency response are actually feasible, or not feasible.

Conflict environments are particularly sensitive. These pre-EMMA 'insights' may be informed by security concerns, or by government policy especially.

It is important to include these perspectives in the market-system selection process, for the same reason as Criterion 3: there is little point in conducting EMMA in a market system if it is known in advance that the recommendations arising from the analysis are unlikely to be implemented.

How to do this

If time is limited, informal discussions among the EMMA team, informed by dialogue with managers, colleagues, and especially staff with local knowledge may be sufficient.

*   If time permits, other agencies and key informants can be invited to participate in a more thorough and formal selection process.
*   Draw on whatever information is available to you from background research, including rapid assessments, livelihood assessments, and household-income surveys, reports on population movements, security updates, government reports, and the seasonal calendar.

Ranking exercises

Ranking exercises may sometimes assist in decision-making. They can also help to explain and summarize to managers or an external audience the rationale for the EMMA team's selection of critical market systems.

In the example in Box 2.9, each 'candidate' market system is given stars to express how strongly it fits each criterion. Remember, however, that these criteria are not objective nor equally important: in the end, EMMA teams must use their best judgement.

Box 2.9 Ranking exercise (example)				
Market-system option:	*A*	*B*	*C*	*D*
1. Relates to significant or urgent need	* *	* *	*	* * *
2. Market system affected by emergency	*	* *	* * *	* *
3. Fits agency mandate well	* *	*	–	* * *
4. Seasonal factors, timing are OK	–	* * *	* *	*
5. Consistent with government or donor plans	* * *	*	*	* *
6. Response options look likely to be feasible	* *	* * *	*	* *
TOTAL	*10*	*12*	*8*	*13*

Consult with colleagues, cluster-group members

Consult management, colleagues, and other humanitarian agencies about the final selection of critical market systems, and the specific objectives or questions (see section 2.4) attached to each of these choices.

It is a good idea to record (and share) the rationale or justification for these choices – by highlighting the criteria that were used or given most weight in the decision process.

EMMA teams should report their provisional decisions to other agencies and key informants, and explain their rationale for each of the selections. UN cluster-group meetings may be an appropriate venue for this kind of information sharing.

In a non-emergency situation, market selection would normally be a participatory process. This is very unlikely to be feasible in most EMMA contexts. However, EMMA teams should grasp any opportunity that may arise to create a simple consultative process with target beneficiaries.

2.4 Specifying the key analytical questions

By now, you will have...
*   identified a short list of critical market systems for EMMA to study;
*   started to establish yourself in the emergency network (e.g. receiving updates from cluster and co-ordination groups);
*   clarified and communicated to your team your agency's mandate and scope of likely responses;
*   begun developing some ideas for possible responses.

As the examples in the the Introduction illustrate, there are various ways in which EMMA can be useful:
*   to compare the wisdom (pros and cons) of direct cash and in-kind responses;
*   to explore opportunities for complementary market-system support actions;
*   to highlight any risks of doing harm (especially in the longer term).

Provided that the selection process was done carefully, it should be possible to identify specific and tangible reasons for applying EMMA in each selected market system. These reasons can usually be expressed as 'key analytical questions' which EMMA aims to answer – see Box 2.10 for examples.

Box 2.10 Key analytical questions (examples)	
Market system	*Key analytical questions*
Timber market system, Haiti, 2008	What capacity does the timber market system have to supply housing-reconstruction materials to the target population? What form of support for accessing timber is preferable: cash grants, relief-agency distributions, or some other? Why?
Beans market system, Haiti, 2008	How has (target group) farmers' access to markets to sell beans been affected by the hurricanes? What is the availability of beans to supply consumption needs of the target population in the affected area? When should existing food aid be phased out, and how?
Fishing-nets market system, Myanmar, 2008	What are the main constraints affecting the re-supply of fishing nets to subsistence fisher-folk (target group) in the delta? What form of assistance to fishing households is most needed? Are there any obvious interventions in the fishing-net supply chain that could speed recovery of this system?

These key questions are vitally important, because they provide the following:

- an easily accessible explanation of EMMA's objectives for managers;
- a means of explaining EMMA to colleagues, key informants, and interviewees;
- a focus for the EMMA team's efforts during fieldwork.

However, don't forget that EMMA is an iterative process. The key questions are not set in stone at this stage: they will most likely change or be added to during Step 3 and again in Step 5.

Livestock and seed systems in emergencies

Comprehensive guidance has recently been published, focusing specifically on livelihood protection in relation to two frequently selected market systems: livestock and seeds. These resources describe the key issues and analytical questions which should inform any EMMA investigations in these systems.

Emergency seed programmes are a potentially complex arena for intervention, since farmers' own seed-replication systems intersect with those of market-based suppliers, and this fact is compounded by concerns about appropriate seed-variety selection and the need to protect bio-diversity. See the CIAT guide to assessing seed-system security that is included in the EMMA reference manual materials (Sperling, 2008).

Comprehensive advice on livestock programming has recently been published in the Sphere-related Livestock Emergency Guidelines and Standards. A useful short review of this LEGS tool is included in the EMMA reference manual materials (Watson and Catley, 2008).

Checklist for Step 2

o   Brainstorm widely the options for market systems to be investigated.

o   Agree criteria for selecting which market systems are most critical.

o   Narrow down the final selection of critical market systems.

o   Identify the key analytical questions for each market system.

STEP 3
Preliminary analysis

Stripping corn in the back yard, Peru. This area is prone to flooding and landslides, as the nearby river may change its course when it rains heavily.

From this point onwards, each critical market system selected for EMMA investigation is mapped and analysed separately. Step 3 involves the first rough-and-ready attempt to describe and sketch the market system – as it was before the crisis, and as it is now. These early iterations will encourage you to define more clearly the key analytical questions that EMMA is aiming to answer, and begin thinking about which informants may provide the necessary information.

> **Before starting Step 3, the EMMA leader should have...**
>
> o   confirmed with the agency the 'terms of reference' of the EMMA investigation;
> o   identified the target population (and groups within it), and their basic priority needs;
> o   decided which market systems are to be the subject of EMMA investigation;
> o   drafted initial versions of the key analytical questions.

3.1 Overview of Step 3

Objectives

- Sketch preliminary maps of the market system in baseline and emergency-affected situations.
- Revise and refine the key analytical questions drafted in Step 2.
- Identify the most promising key informants and market actors to start talking to.

Activities

Section 3.2 : Getting started with mapping
- Familiarize the EMMA field team with the toolkit, concepts, and expected outputs.

Sections 3.3–3.5: Preliminary mapping of the market systems
- Undertake initial mapping of baseline and emergency-affected situations.
- Develop a picture of the different market-system components.

Sections 3.6–3.8: Using the market map to understand the system
- Revise and update the market-system map with more information.
- Compare the baseline and emergency-affected situations.
- Sketch an initial seasonal calendar for the market system.
- Update the key analytical questions.

Key outputs

- Preliminary market maps – baseline and emergency-affected
- Preliminary seasonal calendar for market system
- Revised key analytical questions
- Contacts and leads for key informants.

3.2 Getting started with market mapping

The 'market system' concept

The 'market system' is a crucial idea for EMMA. It means more than simply a market place or a supply chain. It is a way of thinking about the complete web of different actors, structures, and rules which together determine how goods are produced, exchanged, and accessed by different people.

As section 2.2 explained, EMMA applies the concept of a market system independently to particular goods, crops, non-food items, or services. So, for example, EMMA may look separately at the market systems for sorghum, for clothing, and for transport services.

Crucially in EMMA, *target groups are part of market systems*. In almost all situations, ordinary households use markets for acquiring food, items, and services, and for selling their produce and labour. Non-monetary forms of exchange (e.g. reciprocal services) can also be included in the market-system approach. In order to analyse the capacity of market systems to play a role in humanitarian response, it is vital to understand how target groups access and use markets.

Consider, for example, the market system for a staple commodity like rice. This system includes the traders, retailers, and millers who trade in rice. It also includes farmers and agricultural labourers who produce rice; and of course the suppliers of seeds and inputs. It may include government officials who regulate the rice industry. Finally, the system includes rice consumers.

Market-system maps

Market-system mapping is the central tool in EMMA. It is derived from a participatory approach to market development, designed by the international NGO Practical Action (Albu and Griffith, 2005). It emphasizes simple and visually engaging methods of communicating and sharing knowledge about complex systems among non-specialists. Ultimately, its aim is to build up quickly a comprehensive sketch of a market system in its entirety. Market maps can then be used for the following purposes:

- to collate and represent information about market systems during the study;
- to assist comparisons of pre-emergency (baseline) and emergency-affected situations;
- to facilitate discussion, interpretation, and analysis of data within the EMMA team;
- to communicate findings about market systems to others.

In practice, the mapping process is an *iterative* process: it happens incrementally. You will start by doing a preliminary mapping (a rough outline) of each of the critical market systems selected in Step 2. This will initially be based simply on whatever knowledge, however sketchy, the team can immediately marshal. You should then expect to draw and re-draw your maps several times during the course of the EMMA process, so that your initially rough outline gets progressively more detailed as you learn more and more about the system.

> **Box 3.1 Induction for inexperienced EMMA teams**
>
> If you are leading an emergency assessment process with a field team lacking previous experience of EMMA, an early task will be to introduce EMMA concepts and tools. The preliminary mapping activities described in this chapter are a practical and engaging way to explain basic EMMA concepts and introduce the main market tools described in the introductory chapter.
>
> An outline of a short in-country training or induction course for EMMA field teams is included in the EMMA reference manual on CD-ROM. This covers:
> *   EMMA outputs – what the process is aiming to achieve;
> *   EMMA concepts/rationale – what a market system is and why they matter;
> *   Overview of the ten steps of the EMMA process;
> *   Market mapping – a tool for visualizing and analysing market systems;
> *   Fieldwork preparation and practice – developing and testing the fieldwork agenda.

Establishing a baseline

A characteristic feature of the EMMA process is comparison between baseline and emergency-affected situations. In a sudden-onset emergency, the baseline refers to the state of affairs before the crisis struck. It is both a description of the normal 'situation before' and a best guess at the conditions that agencies can realistically expect to prevail when the market system recovers in due course.

As you will see in Step 8, baseline data will be used as a guide to the inherent capabilities and limitations of market-system actors: it can tell us what can be realistically expected from the system. This is crucial if agencies are going to rely on market actors to play their role in humanitarian response.

It is therefore important that any baseline provides a relevant comparison in terms of time (season) and place (geography), to enable the emergency situation to be assessed effectively.

*   *Seasonally*: the baseline should describe the market system as it was during the same time of year (or the same seasonal conditions) as the emergency for which a response is being planned.

    If responses will be implemented during the dry season, the baseline should describe a 'normal' dry-season situation, rather than the market system as it was during the hurricane season that immediately preceded and precipitated the emergency.

*   *Geographically*: the baseline should describe the market system in the location where the emergency response is planned.

    If the target population has moved (i.e. as refugees and displaced people), the most relevant baseline situation will usually be the market system that existed before the emergency, *in their new location*.

Occasionally it is difficult to define an appropriate baseline, because the critical items or goods were not previously traded much in the local economy (e.g. specialist shelter materials). Even when prior market activity was negligible, it is usually possible to trace market links back to some national-level producer or buyer, and describe any relevant infrastructure and services.

Preliminary mapping

The first step in mapping a market system is simply to start drawing. Do not wait until you think you know everything that you want to know. If you are very lucky, background research (Step 1) may have revealed the existence of localized market studies (i.e. describing the emergency zone) available from district government offices or local NGOs. Sometimes government agencies, the World Bank, or NGOs may have completed sub-sector analyses for specific markets that will give you an excellent picture of the baseline situation. However, the general knowledge of EMMA team members and colleagues consulted during the market-selection process (Step 2) is always enough to get started.

For example, Box 3.2 shows an early attempt to describe the baseline market system for fishing nets in Myanmar's Ayeyarwady delta area. This was drawn before fieldwork began. There were many errors, but drawing the map helped the EMMA field team to work out what issues and questions they needed to focus on (their knowledge gaps) when they began interviews.

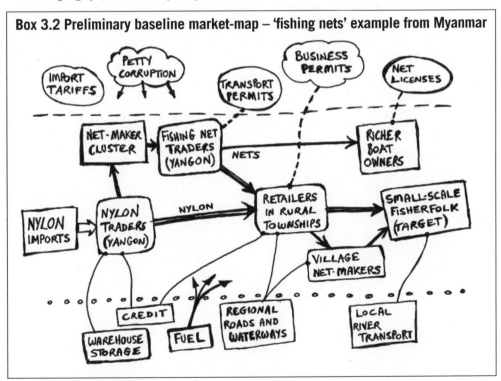

Box 3.2 Preliminary baseline market-map – 'fishing nets' example from Myanmar

Logically it is best to begin mapping the baseline situation first. However, this is not a strict rule: you can also begin with the emergency-affected situation, if this feels more 'natural' to the team.

3.3 Mapping the market chain

The central feature of any market-system map is a 'chain' of different market actors who exchange, buy, and sell goods as the latter move from primary producer to final consumer. These market actors include, for example, small-holder farmers, larger-scale producers, traders, processors, transporters, wholesalers, retailers, and of course consumers.

• In 'supply' market systems, this sequence is sometimes called a *supply chain*.
• In 'income' market systems, the series of actors is often called a *value chain*.

The first task in mapping is to identify the businesses involved in the main chain in the critical market system. Then work out the linkages between them: who sells to whom, and how. See Box 3.3 for an example. Remember to include the target groups in the map – whether they are primary producers, labourers, or consumers.

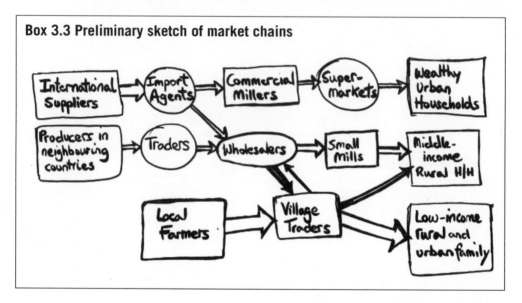

Box 3.3 Preliminary sketch of market chains

Different market chains within one system

In some market systems, you may identify several interacting and *competing* market chains. There may also be more than one identifiable group of final consumers. This level of detail matters if, for example, different target groups obtain their supplies, or market their produce, in ways that are significantly different from each other.

At this early stage, even without detailed information, it may be possible to estimate the relative scale, size, or importance to target groups of different sources of supply, different linkages, or end markets. These can be indicated, for example, by using different *thickness of arrows* and *differently sized boxes*. Think about why some chains are more important than others. Remember, what matters for EMMA is the role (past, existing, or potential) that the market system plays in humanitarian response for the target population.

Identifying target groups on the market map

It is important to include and identify your target groups (section 1.6), in the market map. From a target group's perspective, market chains work in different directions.

- In 'supply' systems, the chains bring in food, items, and services to affected households.
- In 'income' systems, they enable households to earn income through the sale of produce or labour.

In the first case, the target group are actual or potential buyers or consumers of food, items, and services, which the market system supplies through the supply chain (also called a 'pipeline' by logisticians). This applies to food and essential household items (EHI), and also to livelihood inputs and urgently needed livelihood assets.

In the second case, the target groups are producers, workers, or labourers who rely (actually or potentially) on the market system providing income through the value chain. We usually find them towards the beginning of the value chain – but they may also be in the middle (e.g. as factory workers in urban settings).

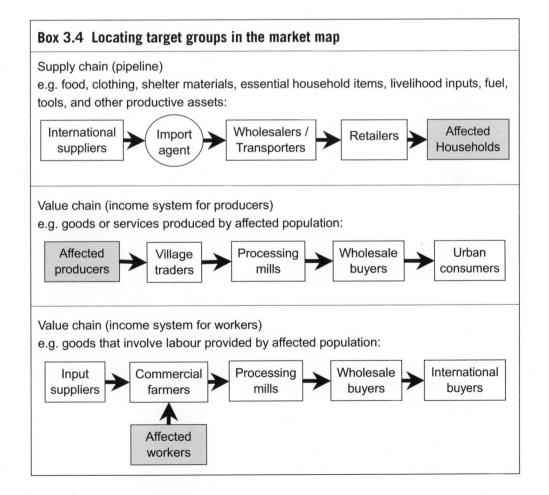

Box 3.4 Locating target groups in the market map

Supply chain (pipeline)
e.g. food, clothing, shelter materials, essential household items, livelihood inputs, fuel, tools, and other productive assets:

International suppliers → Import agent → Wholesalers / Transporters → Retailers → Affected Households

Value chain (income system for producers)
e.g. goods or services produced by affected population:

Affected producers → Village traders → Processing mills → Wholesale buyers → Urban consumers

Value chain (income system for workers)
e.g. goods that involve labour provided by affected population:

Input suppliers → Commercial farmers → Processing mills → Wholesale buyers → International buyers

Affected workers → Commercial farmers

Be alert to the possibility that different target groups play *different roles in the same critical market system*, and therefore will have experienced different kinds of impact from the emergency situation.

Gender roles in market systems

Women and men often have very different roles and responsibilities within any given market system. For example, in staple-food systems, women may be 'producers' in the sense of doing the physical agricultural work, but men may take responsibility for selling any surpluses to traders. Where such gender divisions are strongly present, EMMA users should be cautious about mapping the household as a single market actor. It may be necessary to differentiate between male and female actors, since the impact of the emergency, and their needs and preferences for assistance, cannot be assumed to be the same. Box 3.5 illustrates one way to represent intra-household differences for subsistence producers on a market map.

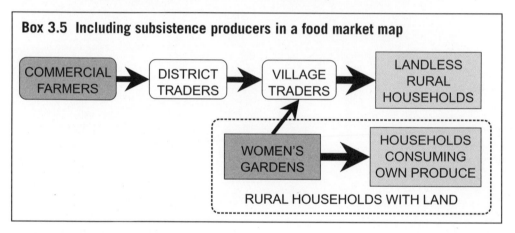

Box 3.5 Including subsistence producers in a food market map

Subsistence producers

The distinction between supply and income systems can seem irrelevant when looking at subsistence agriculture – where households consume most or all of their own food produce – and there may be little 'market' transaction. However, this does not mean that EMMA can ignore the subsistence economy. When subsistence-food production is emergency-affected, EMMA needs to understand the size of the gap that this will create in the overall market system. So, even though there is no market transaction between a subsistence farmer and the household who depend on her produce, it is still vital to include subsistence production and consumption in a food market map.

One way to include subsistence-food producers in a market map is illustrated in Box 3.5. The rural household with land (indicated by dashed-line box) is shown to include both producer and consumer, with a small proportion of its produce sold to village traders.

Seasonal awareness

Seasonal factors may be highly significant in locating some target groups. Where livelihood strategies are seasonally varied, target groups may take the role of producers or labourers at one time of year and the role of consumers during a different season. For example, in market systems for staple food crops, it is common to find households who earn income from agricultural work, or from the sale of surplus production around harvest time, but who are net food consumers and purchasers during the off-peak season.

This means that EMMA practitioners need to refer to the *seasonal calendar*: thinking about when in the seasonal cycle the crisis has happened, and when the response will be implemented. Even in the same market system, very different responses may be appropriate at different times of year. See section 3.8 below.

Market segmentation

EMMA works by analysing each critical market system in an emergency situation separately. However, it is not always easy to clearly define the boundaries of a particular market system. During the fieldwork, you may find that the market system is actually divided into two or more segments due to differences in the quality or brand of the goods being traded. These segments may serve different end-markets.

For example: the market system for a staple crop (e.g. beans) may contain a large segment that is trading in average-quality items, and a separate smaller segment trading in a high-quality variety consumed only by wealthier households.

Box 3.6 Optimal ignorance

'Optimal ignorance' refers to the importance of disregarding non-essential or unnecessary detail. Focus attention only on the most relevant elements of the system. If you find that parts of a market system do not influence access and availability for the target population – i.e. parallel or independent market segments – it may be possible to ignore them.

This requires judgement. It is easy to be diverted down interesting but irrelevant avenues of enquiry, especially if your key informants are enthusiastic about their own areas of knowledge. You must constantly assess the relevance of information that you are hearing and try to ignore the distractions.

In these cases, do not waste time investigating the market segment that is not relevant (Box 3.6) to the target population's needs. Also, avoid mixing up data (prices, volumes) about the 'irrelevant' market segment with the segment that is critical for EMMA, as your results may be distorted as a result.

3.4 Mapping the infrastructure, inputs, and services

The second step of market-system mapping is concerned with the various forms of infrastructure, inputs, and services that support the system's overall functioning. Different actors always depend upon various forms of supporting infrastructure, inputs, and services from other enterprises, organizations, and governments.

Examples of infrastructure and business services include:

- water and electricity utilities;
- input supplies (seeds, livestock, fertilizers, etc.);
- market information services (about prices, trends, buyers, suppliers);
- financial services (such as credit, savings, or insurance);
- transport services and infrastructure;
- technical expertise and business advice.

Identify the most crucial elements of infrastructure and services, and link these to their users within the market system. The aim is to get an overall picture of the role that these services play in maintaining the market system's efficiency and accessibility.

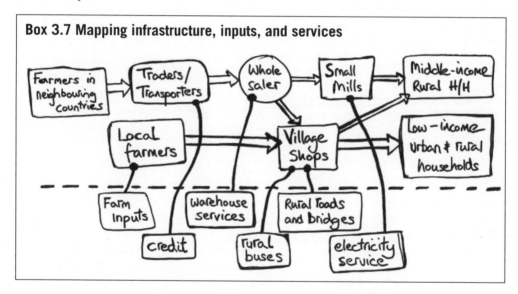

Box 3.7 Mapping infrastructure, inputs, and services

There is often a vast range of these infrastructural and business services, so the mapping task is to identify and focus (i.e. in interviews with traders) on the ones that seem likely to play a really essential role, and / or have been strongly affected by the emergency situation. Try not to overload the map with linkages, but focus on the most salient examples.

3.5 Mapping institutions, rules, norms, and trends

The third step of market-system mapping is concerned with issues and trends that are significant influences on the *market environment* in which producers, traders, and other market actors operate. This environment is shaped by various policies, regulations, social and business practices, and trends.

EMMA is interested in the most important issues which were or are influencing market-system capabilities, efficiency, and equity, before and since the emergency began. Many different types of issue may be worth recording in the market-system map. Even if there is little that humanitarian agencies can do to alter them, an understanding of the constraints that they create should be included in the selection and design of responses. For example:

- weakness in the basic rules and institutions needed to help the market system to work effectively (e.g. contract-enforcement systems, land registries, producer organizations, trading standards);
- official rules and policies – by-laws, licensing regulations, taxes – which hinder and block rather than assist market-system functioning;
- arbitrary small-scale abuses of power by people in roles of authority (corruption and bribery);
- socially enforced roles and rules that obstruct some people from participating in certain kinds of activity, or block their access to markets, on the basis of gender, ethnicity, etc.

Differences in gender roles and responsibilities between women and men are an especially pervasive factor which shapes how market systems operate. These social rules may limit the options for market access or income generation that are open to women, for example.

This component of the market map is also a good place to highlight any major long-term trends that were affecting the market system and target population even before the emergency: for example, economic trends, climate changes, population movements, and natural-resource constraints.

- Environmental trends, such as natural-resource depletion or climate change, that are affecting actors in the market system.
- Economic trends, for example in the international price of the critical food or item, or the value of the local currency.

Add these over-arching 'market-environment' issues to the market map in the same way as the infrastructure and services were added before. If relevant, it may be useful to link the issue identified to specific market actors or chains.

Box 3.8 Mapping the market environment

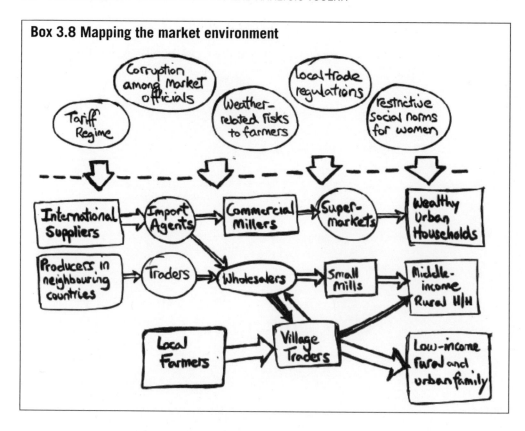

3.6 Developing the market map through further iterations

Within a few hours, EMMA teams should be able to sketch out complete preliminary maps for both the baseline and emergency-affected situations. These preliminary market maps will inevitably change in structure and content throughout the subsequent EMMA steps. For example, see how the preliminary map illustrated in Box 3.2 evolved into the final map shown in Box 3.9.

During the early phases of fieldwork design, the maps will guide you in deciding which market actors or key informants you should meet. The maps will help to reveal gaps in your knowledge of the market system, and thus help you to develop your interview agenda and questionnaires (Step 4).

In key-informant and field interviews (Step 5), you will learn and include more information about volumes, prices of commodities, and numbers of market actors. You will probably be updating your market maps on a daily basis during the fieldwork, as new information is obtained (Step 6).

Detailed analysis of these maps will be done in Step 8, where we look at possible response options.

Comparing baseline and emergency-affected maps

As soon as you have a preliminary draft map, it is possible to begin recording the impact of the crisis. Examples of impacts may include the following:

*   the disappearance of some market actors;
*   partial or complete disruption to some linkages or relationships in the chain;
*   damage to infrastructure, and blockage of services;
*   new relationships or linkages formed as coping strategies by market actors;
*   changes in the relative importance of different linkages (i.e. volume of trade);
*   introduction of new supply channels (e.g. aid distributions).

These impacts – which are still very possibly speculative at this early stage – can be indicated on a market map, using simple visual 'flags' to highlight various kinds of disruption to market actors, functions, and linkages in the system (see Box 3.10).

3.
Preliminary
analysis

Box 3.9 Final baseline market map – 'fishing nets' example from Myanmar

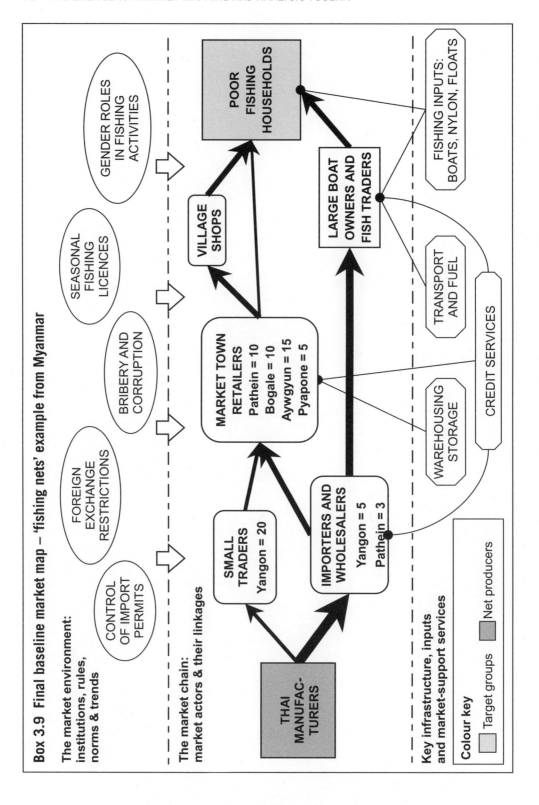

The market environment: institutions, rules, norms & trends

CONTROL OF IMPORT PERMITS

FOREIGN EXCHANGE RESTRICTIONS

BRIBERY AND CORRUPTION

SEASONAL FISHING LICENCES

GENDER ROLES IN FISHING ACTIVITIES

The market chain: market actors & their linkages

POOR FISHING HOUSEHOLDS

VILLAGE SHOPS

MARKET TOWN RETAILERS
Pathein = 10
Bogale = 10
Aywgyun = 15
Pyapone = 5

SMALL TRADERS
Yangon = 20

IMPORTERS AND WHOLESALERS
Yangon = 5
Pathein = 3

THAI MANUFACTURERS

LARGE BOAT OWNERS AND FISH TRADERS

FISHING INPUTS: BOATS, NYLON, FLOATS

TRANSPORT AND FUEL

WAREHOUSING STORAGE

CREDIT SERVICES

Key infrastructure, inputs and market-support services

Colour key

Target groups

Net producers

Box 3.10 Final emergency-affected market map – 'fishing nets' example from Myanmar

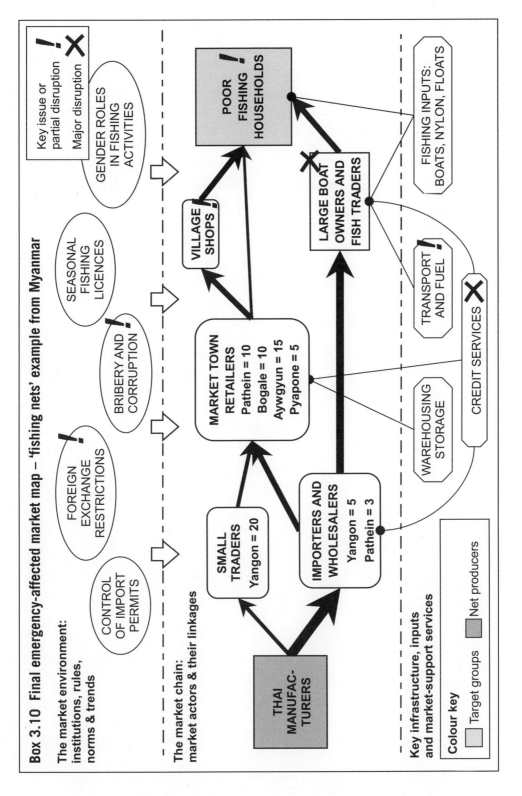

The market environment:
institutions, rules, norms & trends

CONTROL OF IMPORT PERMITS

FOREIGN EXCHANGE RESTRICTIONS !

BRIBERY AND CORRUPTION !

SEASONAL FISHING LICENCES

GENDER ROLES IN FISHING ACTIVITIES

Key issue or partial disruption !

Major disruption ✕

The market chain:
market actors & their linkages

POOR FISHING HOUSEHOLDS !

VILLAGE SHOPS !

LARGE BOAT OWNERS AND FISH TRADERS ✕

MARKET TOWN RETAILERS
Pathein = 10
Bogale = 10
Aywgyun = 15
Pyapone = 5

SMALL TRADERS
Yangon = 20

IMPORTERS AND WHOLESALERS
Yangon = 5
Pathein = 3

THAI MANUFAC-TURERS

Key infrastructure, inputs and market-support services

FISHING INPUTS: BOATS, NYLON, FLOATS

TRANSPORT AND FUEL !

CREDIT SERVICES ✕

WAREHOUSING STORAGE

Colour key

Target groups

Net producers

3. Preliminary analysis

3.7 Preliminary seasonal calendar for market system

As noted above, many market systems have strong seasonal variations in the patterns of production, trade, and prices. These patterns may reveal themselves through seasonal price fluctuations for inputs and outputs. Or they may involve major seasonal shifts of activity as people move, for example, between farming and wage employment.

This is most obvious in agricultural market systems, with shifts in demand for labour for ploughing, weeding, and harvesting, and a surge in the supply of produce after harvesting. However, seasonal patterns may also feature in shelter-related markets, and in off-farm activities that are affected by weather or road access, for example.

It is essential that EMMA users are able to distinguish between 'normal' seasonal fluctuations in prices and trade volumes and the disruptions created by an emergency situation. Otherwise, your diagnosis of market-system problems and proposed solutions will be flawed. The baseline market map should represent a 'seasonally relevant' picture.

It is a good idea, therefore, to begin constructing a preliminary version of a seasonal calendar (Box 3.11) for each market system analysed, to capture the 'normal' seasonal patterns of price and trade. As more information becomes available, this can also be used to describe other important features of the system which may be relevant to the humanitarian response.

Box 3.11 Seasonal calendar for market system												
Factor	*S*	*O*	*N*	*D*	*J*	*F*	*M*	*A*	*M*	*J*	*J*	*A*
Prices of item	Low								High			
Trade volumes	High									Low		
Employment level			Planting: high				Low			Harvest		
Input purchases				$					$			
Main harvest sale												
Repayments due	$	$										
Flooding season						Flood						

3.8 Revising EMMA's key analytical questions

The preliminary market maps and seasonal calendars – however sketchy and incomplete – are first steps in the iterative process that leads to robust response recommendations. Similarly, the key questions that you identified after the market-system selection (section 2.4) will also evolve and change as you develop your understanding of the situation.

The final activity in Step 3 is to reflect on the preliminary maps, and ask yourself the following questions:

- How does the target population interact with this market system?
- What are the most important channels and actors in the system – likely focal points for enquiries, points of leverage?
- What has been the impact of the crisis?
- What do we not know, and need to know?

Ask yourself who is likely to be able to answer these questions. Who are likely to be the most useful key informants, especially to begin with? These are likely to be larger market actors (e.g. wholesalers) who have an overview of the market system as a whole, including the roles of services (such as finance, transport), policy, and regulation.

You should also think about government officials, the managers of local NGOs, and sector specialists who can help EMMA teams to build up a general preliminary understanding of the market system and the emergency situation.

Checklist for Step 3

o   Introduce the EMMA field team to basic concepts and mapping techniques.

o   Sketch preliminary baseline and emergency-affected market maps.

o   Sketch a preliminary seasonal calendar for the market system.

o   Revise key analytical questions, in light of better understanding of system.

STEP 4
Preparation for fieldwork

Photo credit: Jim Holmes

4.
Fieldwork
preparation

The bridge near Lamno, in Aceh Province, Indonesia, has survived for over a year now, hand-built by villagers from coconut palms felled in the tsunami.

Step 4 develops the questions, interview plans, and information-recording formats needed for EMMA interviews and other fieldwork. A mixture of qualitative information and quantitative data will be sought through fieldwork that is rapid, informal, and often conducted in local languages. EMMA interviews need to be planned so as to avoid rigid structures and encourage easy flow of communication.

Before starting Step 4, the EMMA leader should have...

o   drawn up a preliminary list of likely information sources (market actors, key informants, locations);
o   acquired basic interview skills and an understanding of EMMA's aims, tools, and concepts;
o   sketched preliminary market maps (showing baseline and emergency-affected situations);
o   refined the key analytical questions that EMMA is seeking to answer.

4.1 Overview of Step 4

Objectives

- Develop a set of focused interview agendas relevant to the specific market system.
- Write structured interview questions for each category of informant.
- Tailor response forms to assist in recording quantitative data and qualitative information.
- Refresh interview techniques and fieldwork skills of the EMMA team.

Activities

Sections 4.2–4.5: Interview agendas
- Identify the information needs that arise in each EMMA strand.
- Translate these into interview questions that can be used in the field.

Sections 4.6–4.7: Special issues in the fieldwork agenda
- Gender, conflict situations, transport, and financial services
- Cash-feasibility questions

Sections 4.8–4.9: Preparation and rehearsal
- Testing and rehearsal of interview formats
- Preparation of data-sheets

Key outputs

- Interview structures and questionnaires for different types of market actor and other informant
- Data sheets to record and collate quantitative data

4.2 EMMA's fieldwork agenda

The fieldwork agenda is a list of the issues or questions that the EMMA team is trying to answer. Market systems are often rather complex, as you may have already discovered from the preliminary mapping exercise in Step 3. It is therefore essential that the fieldwork agenda is carefully planned and as tightly focused as possible, given your knowledge of the situation.

The starting point must be the key analytical questions already drafted in Steps 2 and 3. More generally, EMMA teams will be interested in issues such as the following:
- Are emergency needs likely to be better met by cash-based interventions or by distributions of items?
- Does the local market system have the capacity to meet the emergency needs of the target affected population if their purchasing power is increased (e.g. by cash-based intervention)?

- What is the likely impact of any proposed cash-based or in-kind intervention on markets (including the likelihood of high or prolonged price distortions)?
- What are the key interventions to rehabilitate and ensure more long-term stability in market systems for critical food or non-food consumption, or in market systems that provide employment?
- How to ensure that emergency interventions are designed to support (and not undermine) existing long-term interventions?
- What are the key market indicators to be monitored throughout the course of an intervention?

As the introductory chapter described (section 0.4), EMMA breaks this investigation agenda down into three strands:

1. *Gap-analysis (or 'People') strand.* Understanding the emergency situation, priority needs, and preferences of the target population. It also puts these women's and men's needs (the gaps or deficits that they face) in the context of their economic profile and livelihood strategies.
2. *Market-system analysis strand.* Understanding the market system's constraints and capabilities in terms of playing a role in the emergency response. It develops a map and profile of the (pre-crisis) baseline situation and explores the impact of the emergency on it.
3. *Response-analysis strand.* Exploring different options and opportunities for humanitarian agencies. It looks at each option's respective feasibility, likely outcomes, benefits, and risks, before leading to recommendations for action.

The next sections examine the fieldwork agenda for each of these strands in turn.

4.3 The gap-analysis agenda

The basic fieldwork objectives in this strand are as follows:
- To verify your understanding of livelihood strategies and seasonal factors for women and men in different target groups.
- To confirm and quantify high-priority un-met needs of target-group households.
- To examine any constraints on women's and men's access to markets.
- To investigate different target groups preferences for assistance.

Remember, this is not a general emergency needs assessment, which should have taken place before Step 2. You have already selected the market system to be investigated. Your agenda should focus on the different target groups' interaction with, access to, and use of this specific market system.

In order to make full sense of the information needs listed below, it is essential to study the process described in Step 7 and understand how this information will be used in the gap analysis.

Information needs in gap analysis

- Which groups and how many people normally used (had access to) the market system? Who was included and who was excluded? What are the costs of access (e.g. transport)?
- Were there ever convenient markets for women and men in the area for the critical items? How have different target groups' physical access to the market system been affected?
- What (in income systems) has been the emergency impact in terms of income – wage rates, amount of work, loss of earnings, and hence household budgets? How has this differed for women and men?
- What (in supply systems) has been the impact in terms of reduced consumption or changes in household expenditure? How has this differed for women and men?
  Ultimately, the ideal objective is to be able to construct approximate income and expenditure profiles that show how households, women, and men are adapting to the emergency (Box 4.1).
- What coping mechanisms have women and men adopted since the crisis?
- Do different target groups have strong preferences for the type of assistance that they receive (e.g. cash-based or in-kind assistance), and why?
- What other factors affect / are likely to affect the access of different groups to this market system (e.g. gender roles, distance from trading posts, social or ethnic obstacles)?
- Are there any critical issues of accessibility that need to be factored into the analysis of the situation? How do these affect men and women differently?

Box 4.1 Information about household expenditure

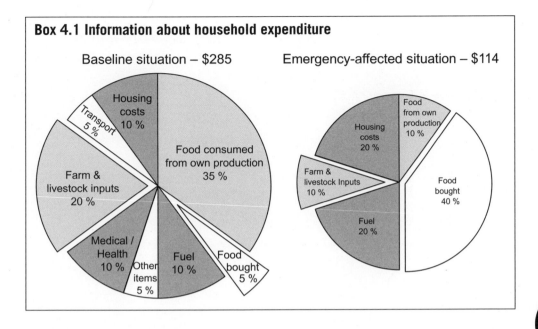

Baseline situation – $285

Emergency-affected situation – $114

4.4 The market-analysis agenda

The basic fieldwork objectives in this strand are as follows:

- To investigate the structure and conduct of the market system prior to the crisis.
- To obtain data about 'normal' production and trade volumes, prices in the pre-crisis baseline situation.
- To explore the impact of the crisis on market actors, infrastructure, and services, and understand their coping strategies.
- To assess (quantify) production and trade volumes, stocks, and prices since the crisis began.
- To identify current and expected constraints on the market system's performance in near future.

This agenda is the core of the EMMA toolkit – which distinguishes it from existing humanitarian assessment tools. Because market systems are often complex and hard to understand in their entirety, the market-system maps are crucial in identifying the most important information needs. You should use the preliminary maps as a tool for focusing attention on the market-system components and features that are most relevant to the target population. This must be an iterative process, since the EMMA team's awareness of what aspects of the system are salient may initially be low. As your understanding of the system grows during the fieldwork (Step 5), you may well need to re-focus your list of information needs and revise the questions that you are putting to informants.

In order to make full sense of the information needs listed below, it is essential to study the market-analysis process described in Steps 6 and 8, and understand how this information will be used in market mapping and analysis steps.

Information needs in market analysis

Market-chain actors and linkages

- Who were the market-chain actors, and how were they interlinked within the market system? What functions (roles) did different market actors play in the supply chain?
- How many compete to perform any specific function at different points in the system?
- What impact has the emergency had on particular market-chain actors and their linkages or relationships? Have specific functions in the market system been affected?
- What have traders or other market actors done to cope with or respond to the impacts listed above? In their view, why are goods available, or not available?

Infrastructure, inputs, and services

- What services and infrastructure played a part in supporting the market system (e.g. input suppliers, market information, transport, storage, technical expertise, financial services, etc.)?
- What impact has the emergency had on services and infrastructure which normally support the market system?

Institutions, rules, regulations, and norms

- What institutions, rules, regulations, and norms played an important part in shaping the business environment for this market system (either positively or negatively)?
- What impact (either positive or negative) has the emergency had on institutions, rules, regulations, and norms that normally shape the business environment for this market system?

Quantities and prices

- What volumes / quantities would normally be traded (at this time of year)?
- What prices (at various points in the system, e.g. import, wholesale, retail) would be normal?
- What has happened to stocks, quantities available and supplied, since the crisis began?
- How long does it take traders to order or re-stock goods for sale?

- What has happened to prices – at key points in the supply chain or value chain – since the crisis began?
- How do prices compare with a normal year? With import-parity prices? What is the trend? What predictions are people making about future price trends?

Seasonality

- How does trade change during the year (i.e. religious holidays, production, road conditions, transport costs, crop calendar, etc.)?
- When are seasonal variations in access, prices, variety, and quantities experienced?

Competition / market power

- Are there functions (or links) in the market system which are normally dominated by one or two traders alone, such that they can control prices? Or do traders compete with each other?
- To what extent have the crisis and its outcomes undermined competition or created imbalances of market power in the market system?

Market integration

- From where do traders normally purchase goods brought into the local area? Is there normally significant trading between the crisis-affected area and other less-affected areas?
- Do seasonal price fluctuations in the local area normally reflect similar fluctuations in the national market?
- Can the local market easily be reached by suppliers and purchasers?
- To what extent have the crisis and its outcomes reduced integration with neighbouring markets?

4.5 The response-analysis agenda

The basic fieldwork objectives in this strand are as follows:
- To identify any plausible support actions to rapidly assist coping, recovery, or better performance of the market system.
- To collect any other information that indicates the operational feasibility of various response options being proposed by respondents.

In order to make full sense of the information needs listed below, it is essential to study the response-analysis process described in Step 9, and understand how this information will be used in response analysis.

Information needs in response analysis

- What are the main constraints on the market system's role in emergency response?
- What are the immediate and longer-term actions that might be undertaken to remedy the situation?
- How quickly could these interventions be implemented, so as to be relevant?
- What resources would be required to implement each approach?
- What are the existing structure(s) that can be worked with (i.e. unions, guilds, associations, NGOs, local groups, lending institutions, networks, government agencies, etc.)?
- How feasible is it in technical, social, and political terms to deliver each of these support options in practice?

4.6 Special issues in market-system analysis

Impacts on particular market actors, system linkages, and relationships

Look for damage to particular types of business in the supply chain or value chain. Focus on impacts on business linkages or trading relationships that are causing the greatest disruption to the overall system from the point of view of the target population (as households, producers, or workers).

Loss of business assets, premises, vehicles, and stocks for some types of market actor (e.g. wholesalers, land-owners) may have a particularly severe impact on the market system as a whole. Look out for compounding problems. For example, if shop keepers are the main source of credit, the destruction of shops may be a double blow to affected households.

Economic catchment areas

When quantifying production and trade volumes, it is essential to define the economic area to which the data refer. This might be the local emergency zone itself, the wider district or a region that is the main source of supplies, or the national picture. The reason for this is explained in Step 8.

Often, there can be no objective definition of the boundaries of the 'local economic area'. However, local traders will usually be able to explain to you what they regard as their territory. This may be determined by local geography (a valley, an island), or by the economic catchment area of a particular market town or city.

Impacts on services and infrastructure

Find out about any damage to vital services (e.g. transport, communications, finance, animal health) that were important to the effective performance of the market system in the baseline situation. Record what has happened to the providers of these services, and the prospects for their recovery.

Consider also any essential public infrastructure upon which the market system depended heavily in the baseline situation (e.g. roads, waterways, ports and docks, telephone and electricity grids, water supplies, storage facilities). Record how these have been affected, and what prospects there are for their rehabilitation.

Take note of the plans of local or national governments, or other agencies that are likely to undertake repair of essential infrastructure.

Transport services

Transport is not often seen as a priority emergency need, but transport services play a crucial role in supporting supply chains and value chains in many different market systems. Transport matters not only for the movement of food or goods in supply chains, but also to enable affected people to move to places of work, or find family members. The cross-cutting nature of transport may justify treating transport services as a market system worthy of EMMA investigation in their own right.

Financial services

Financial services are always a key issue in market analysis. Although formal banking services may be rare, there are usually non-formal credit arrangements between market actors, and with consumers, in most market systems. These are easily disrupted in crises, and often slow to recover because of the inter-dependency between actors along a market chain. For example, a retailer who has lost her store in a flood may be unable to re-stock because her customers are also unable to repay her for inputs that they took on credit before the crisis. The situation will be even worse if her wholesaler is also suffering a 'credit crunch'.

EMMA teams need to try to understand the financial relationships among market actors, which are just as relevant as the physical logistics of production and trade. Sometimes these relationships are well suited to rapid and far-reaching emergency response using financial resources (see sections 9.3 and 9.4).

See Minimum Standards for Economic Recovery After Crisis (SEEP Network, 2009).

Changes to institutions, rules, and norms

Investigate any policies, regulations, social norms, or business practices that have an important influence on how the market system works – in both positive and negative ways. The emergency situation may have exposed the importance of some of these factors; or it may have prompted changes in rules.

Government policies and regulations may be seen to have an especially important influence on the emergency situation; for example:

- restrictions and tariffs on the movement and trade in staple food crops;

- constraints on the economic activities of refugees – employment, land-ownership, etc.

Such policies might be the target for selective lobbying by humanitarian agencies.

Gender roles and norms

Social or cultural norms that govern how different groups or sexes access and use markets or participate in certain forms of employment may, in an emergency context, become a cause of humanitarian concern.

Emergencies have different impacts on women and men. For example, the burden of caring for sick or injured relatives may prevent women from taking advantage of economic opportunities during a crisis. Responsibilities for scavenging food or fuel tend to fall on women – meaning less time for economic activities. Insecurity, and the threat of gender-based violence, may have a huge impact on how, when, and where women can engage with market systems.

It is vital to register these factors in the market mapping and analysis.

Effects of humanitarian action

Do not overlook the effects (impacts) that humanitarian actions may also be having now or in the near future on the market system; or future effects that can be foreseen from planned interventions. Sometimes these post-crisis impacts are just as significant as the shock of the initial crisis. It may be important to include these sorts of activity and effect in your analysis. For example:

- Large-scale food distributions may put traders and retailers out of business.
- Cash-for-work programmes may reduce the availability of labour for local employment.

Market systems in conflict situations

Conflict situations usually lead to very profound disruptions to the rules and norms that operate in market systems and enable them to function effectively. Violence, or the threat of violence, is frequently used to create new relationships of market power that affect issues of who can trade with whom, when, and where. New transaction costs are imposed – for example, through road-blocks and rent-seeking. Sometimes entire parallel or shadow market systems emerge to control trade in lucrative goods: this can be one of the drivers of conflict in the first place.

See the EMMA reference manual for further reading on markets and conflict; also Jaspars and Maxwell (2009), and the Microlinks web link in Box 1.2

4.7 Cash-feasibility agenda

One purpose of EMMA is to help humanitarian managers to decide where cash-based interventions are an appropriate component of emergency response. This decision has both analytical and operational aspects. From a market-analysis perspective, in Steps 8 and 9 you will assess the market system's capacity to respond to the extra demand that cash would stimulate. From an operational perspective, if cash programmes look like a distinct possibility, it is important to include questions (see Box 4.2) about their operational feasibility in the EMMA fieldwork agenda.

Box 4.2 'Operational' questions about cash feasibility

Needs and preferences
- To what extent did women and men depend on cash before the shock?
- What strategies are households using to cope with food or income insecurity?
- Do emergency-affected populations have a preference for cash or in-kind approaches?

Social relations (power differences within households and the community)
- Do men and women have different priorities?
- How is control over resources managed within households?
- What are the differences within the community in terms of control over resources?
- What impact will cash distributions have on existing social and political divisions?

Policy
- What is government policy regarding use of cash-based interventions?

Security and delivery mechanisms
- What are the options for delivering cash to people?
- Are banking systems or informal financial transfer mechanisms functioning?
- What are the risks of cash benefits being taxed or seized by elites or warring parties?
- How do these risks compare with the risks posed by in-kind alternatives to cash?

Corruption
- What are the risks of cash being diverted by local elites or project staff?
- How do these compare with the risks of providing in-kind alternatives?
- What accountability safeguards are available to minimize these risks?

Intervention history
- Have any cash-based interventions been implemented previously in the area?
- What was the outcome? Where there any particular problems? Or positive recommendations from the experience?

Source: Creti and Jaspars, 2006

**4.
Fieldwork
preparation**

4.8 Interview planning and rehearsal

Matching information needs and sources

Before designing interview structures and devising questionnaires, it is essential to think carefully about the various sources of information and data that you may be consulting in Step 5. They should be a diverse range of individuals: for example, members of target households, petty traders, shop keepers, employers, government officials, wholesalers, import–export agents, local NGO staff, bank officials.

For each type of respondent or informant, the EMMA team must consider the following:

- the type of information (gap, market, response) which each informant is most likely to be able to supply;
- the amount of time available and, hence, the number of questions you will have an opportunity to ask;
- the language and style of questioning that are appropriate to that individual or group.

Remember to keep the key analytical questions prominently in mind. The information agendas listed above are very intense, and it will usually be unrealistic to try to cover all the issues. You will have to adapt your interview questions and methods to fit your informants. Generally, there are four categories of informant (see Box 4.3).

Box 4.3 Categories of informant, and interview style	
Source of information	*Focus and method of interview*
Target-group households (women and men) (the intended final beneficiaries of emergency response)	Semi-formal questionnaire, narrowly focused gap-analysis issues. Use simple, direct questions in vernacular language. May be conducted with individuals or small groups. Guide time: 20–30 minutes. Interview women separately from men, if possible.
Local market actors *in supply chains* (shop keepers, petty traders, input suppliers, transporters) *in value chains* (employers, buyers, traders)	Structured interview, focusing on the most tangible market-analysis and response-analysis issues. Concentrate on practical information and data about market chain, services, and inputs: prices, volumes, availability, constraints, coping strategies. Include road-side conversations and walk-through meetings. Use simple, direct questions in vernacular language. Ask open questions to allow for qualitative answers as well as quantitative data. Usually on individual basis, 20–40 minutes.
Larger market actors (importers, wholesalers, manufacturers, industrial processors, service providers)	Structured interview, focusing on more strategic market-analysis and response-analysis issues. Concentrate on open-ended 'big picture' questions to understand the system as a whole, especially market shares, trends, and availability. Individual basis, 30 minutes.
Key informants (government officials, NGO staff, chambers of commerce, consultants)	Structured interview, focusing on system-wide issues from across the fieldwork agenda, especially looking at policy issues, rules, and norms. Up to 60 minutes, depending on the individual.

4.
Fieldwork
preparation

Interview structures and questionnaires

Interview structures and questions are generally most effective when prepared, practised, and revised beforehand. When preparing questionnaires, use open-ended and non-leading questions. In general, questions that encourage people to reflect and reveal details are best. Avoid 'closed questions' that prompt simple Yes/No responses, and 'leading questions' that simply invite people to confirm your own assumptions.

Questionnaires generally work best when questions are organized in a logical and categorized manner. You should prepare your questions to follow a flow from one topic to another, allowing the interviewee to remain focused. Bear in mind EMMA's key analytical questions to keep the interview focused on your main goal.

You will need to prepare questionnaires for the unique context of the market system that you are investigating. You will usually need to develop different questionnaires for each category of informant. Boxes 4.4–4.7 provide sample questions. However, it is important to appreciate that in most fieldwork situations EMMA teams will not have sufficient time to cover as many questions as this in every interview. The art of doing fieldwork effectively in emergencies lies in selecting which questions to ask, taking into account the following factors:

- Time available for interviews is always less than ideal, especially with busy market actors and officials.
- Individuals may be (understandably) reluctant to provide some types of information.
- The way in which questions are phrased or presented needs to be sensitive to the type of informant – his or her language, education, and current situation.
- The most pertinent questions to ask will depend on what you already know.

EMMA teams must therefore prepare a flexible set of questions or interview formats for each category of informant. This will need to be reviewed and revised on a daily basis. The tools will evolve iteratively as the fieldwork progresses.

Testing the interview format and questions

If possible, you should test interview structures and questions during the first week of EMMA – even if this means interviewing a few traders outside the emergency area – so that the team have an opportunity to reflect on the results before going to the field (see also section 5.2). This exercise can be integrated into the induction of local EMMA teams, and also provides an opportunity to check and revise their interview techniques.

4.9 Sample questions

Box 4.4 Sample questions for women and men in target households

Your situation in recent 'normal' times (e.g. this same season, but last year)

1.   What were the main foodstuffs (cereals, meat, fish, oil, and vegetables) that your household consumed?
2.   How did you obtain these basic foodstuffs? (*e.g. own production [agriculture, fishing, livestock], purchased in market, collected wild food, gifts from family, barter labour for food, food aid*)
3.   What were the most essential non-food items or other services (*e.g. transport, loans*) that your household used?
4.   What were your primary sources of cash income (or benefits in kind) at this time of year? (*e.g. wage labour, sale of crops, livestock, micro-enterprise activities, remittances*)

Food situation now

5.   How is your household's normal food consumption being affected by the emergency situation? Which of the different foods (above) are affected?
6.   How big is the gap (deficit) that you are now facing in each of these basic food items?
7.   In each case, in what way is the emergency having an impact on your normal consumption? (*e.g. destroyed your crop, reduced your income, raised prices, reduced availability in market, blocked your access to market*)

Essential non-food items or other services now

8.   Which of the essential non-food items and services (above) that your household normally uses have been affected by the emergency situation?
9.   In each case, in what way has the emergency had an impact on your normal usage? (*e.g. increased your need, reduced your income, raised prices, reduced availability in market, blocked your access to market*)
10. What other urgent non-food or service needs do you now have as a result of the emergency situation?

Income and/or employment situation now

11. If you normally rely on casual labour or employment for income, please describe any changes in the amount of work that you are able to find currently; and/or the wage rates.
12. If you normally rely on selling your own produce (food, livestock, manufactured goods) for income, please describe any changes in the amount that you are able to sell, and/or the prices that you obtain.
13. In each case, tell us in what way the emergency is having an effect on your normal earnings / income. (*e.g. made you unable to work, reduced demand for labour, reduced demand for produce, cut transport to jobs, reduced wage rates, reduced selling prices for your goods, changes in the way time is allocated to paid and unpaid activities*)

**4.
Fieldwork
preparation**

Humanitarian response

14. How are you and your household coping? What changes have you and your family made to adjust to the new hardships?
15. Have any agencies intervened to alleviate the situation yet? What activities are offered by the government or NGOs to help you through this time?
16. If you were given cash rather than material aid, what types of goods or services would you purchase first? Where could you spend? Given a choice, how would you prefer to receive assistance with your household food needs? (*e.g. food distributions, cash-based help*)
17. Given a choice, how would you prefer to receive assistance with your household non-food needs? (*e.g. item distributions, cash-based help*)

Box 4.5 Sample questions for local market actors

Your business

1. How is your business doing? What is the impact of the crisis on your business? How do traders and community usually cope in difficult times / how are they managing now?
2. Which products / items are you selling since the crisis began? How much / how many?
3. How much / many would you normally expect to sell at this time of year?
4. What level of stocks are you holding? Is this more or less than normal for you?

Your customers / buyers

5. Who are your customers? What are their characteristics? (NB: 'customer' means person who buys from you, not necessarily the end-user)
6. How many customers do you have these days? (*e.g. number of transactions per week*)
7. How many sales did you have at a similar time of year before the crisis?
8. How has the crisis affected your customers' demand for particular products / items?
9. What is your selling price now? What was your selling price this time last year?

Credit / debt

10. Before the crisis did you normally give any of your customers credit?
11. Are you allowing any of your customers to pay later (have credit) now?
12. How much in total are you owed by your customers? (How many weeks of income?)
13. Before the crisis did you normally get any credit from your suppliers?
14. Are you still able to get credit from your suppliers?
15. How much do you owe your suppliers? (How many weeks' supply?)

Your suppliers

16. Who and where are your suppliers?
17. Has this changed since the crisis began?
18. Are they any seasonal factors affecting prices and affecting when you buy inputs / supplies?
19. Have your suppliers' prices changed since the crisis began? By how much?
20. If demand from your customers increased, how quickly could you supply a) the same quantity as before; b) double the quantity; c) three times as much?
21. Do you think you would have to pay more than before to get these supplies / inputs?

Your business costs (i.e. transport, storage, rents, etc.)

22. What are the major costs that you incur in your business apart from purchasing supplies? (*e.g. transport, storage, premises, labour, licences*)
23. What impact has the crisis had on these costs?

Your competitors (other businesses)

24. How many other businesses (traders) are selling your particular products / items in the same local area as you?
25. What do you estimate is your 'share' of the total market in the area that you serve?
26. Are there any areas nearby that are not getting regular market supplies? If so, why?

The future

27. What are the main problems that you face in doing business now?
28. Are there any restrictions on where you can move goods for sale or buy goods? Market regulations? Which of these problems is related to the impact of the crisis?
29. What do you think could be done to solve any of these problems (especially those related to impact of the crisis)? What are the potential immediate and longer-term steps that can be taken to remedy the situation?

**4.
Fieldwork
preparation**

Box 4.6 Sample questions for larger market actors / key informants

Baseline situation: normal structure and functioning of this market system

Market actors

1. Describe the functional steps and people or companies involved in getting this product to market (i.e. from producers via traders and intermediaries to consumers).
2. What functions does each of these people or companies perform in the chain?
3. What in a normal year are typical prices paid along the market chain at this time of year?

Service providers

4. Are there any important services provided by other businesses which support or make this market chain viable? (*e.g. input suppliers, transport services, storage facilities, communications, financial services*)
5. Are there any important services or infrastructure provided by government / local authorities which support or make this market chain viable? (*e.g. credit facilities, power and water, market places*)

Institutions, rules, and norms

6. What laws, formal rules, or regulations have a big influence (positive or negative) on the way this supply chain works?
7. Are there any informal customs, habits, and practices that shape the relationships (e.g. build trust) between market actors? (*e.g. customs about whom to sell to or buy from*)

Baseline performance of the market system

8. Which are the months of highest demand in a 'typical' year? And lowest demand?
9. Please estimate the total combined local production that you and your competitors traded last season (nationally and in the crisis-affected area).
10. Does the price of this product change seasonally? What time of year are the highest and lowest prices usually? What would normally be the price at this time of year?
11. How much stock is generally available in a normal year? (Breakdown by total stock and in warehouse depots up-country.)
12. Who normally buys your products – rich people, middle-class people, poor people? Could you estimate how much each of these households would typically consume per week?

Is this market usually competitive and well integrated?

13. Are there any points in the supply chain where one or two market actors (e.g. traders) are able to dominate or control the supply and thus set the price of goods?
14. Does the pattern of seasonal price variations in the affected area tend to be the same as the pattern in other regions or in the capital (after accounting for transport costs)? If not, why do you think seasonal price variations in this area are different from elsewhere?

Emergency-affected situation

How has the emergency affected the functioning of the market?

15. What impacts / changes have there been in the supply routes from producer via trader to consumer?
16. Have any particular market actors or functions in the value chain been especially affected?
17. How has the emergency affected important business services mentioned above, important government services, or public infrastructure?
18. How much more costly is it to do business as a result of the emergency? Which business costs have increased (*e.g. fuel, storage, goods, labour, etc.*), and by how much?
19. Have your sales increased or decreased? If so, why?
20. What has happened to your access to local production?
21. Has the emergency affected your ability to import? (*e.g. damage to ports, rail, roads, or lack of customs staff to clear goods*)
22. Have prices for this product increased, decreased, or stayed the same, compared with the normal trends for this time of year? Specify by how much.
23. How much stock of these goods is currently available? Breakdown by total stock and in warehouse depots up-country, especially in disaster-affected area?
24. Are certain groups of consumer now effectively unable to purchase these goods because of high prices or lack of access to suppliers?

How are you dealing with the emergency?

25. How have you adapted your normal trading pattern to overcome challenges caused by the emergency?
26. How well have other actors in the market chain (*e.g. input suppliers, transporters, producers, etc.*) adapted also?

How has the emergency affected competition?

27. Has the emergency affected the way in which supplies and prices are controlled – and if so, how? (*e.g. by reducing the number of businesses in operation, or limiting transport options*)
28. Do you think your largest competitor has enough leverage to restrict supply and drive up prices now?

What if the purchasing power of affected households were restored?

29. If greater demand in the emergency zone were guaranteed, to what extent would you be able to increase your supplies / business volumes in the affected area?
30. Where would you source extra supplies if necessary?
31. Which factors would be most likely to limit your capacity to increase volumes of business?
32. How long would it take you to scale up your trade to meet increased demand?
33. Would there still be certain groups of consumer who would be difficult to supply – for example because of high risks, weak infrastructure, poor roads?

**4.
Fieldwork
preparation**

Box 4.7 Sample questions for large employers

Baseline: normal structure and functioning of this market system

Value-chain actors

1. What is the nature of your business (production of goods or services) and what are its inputs? Who is involved in delivering your raw materials, etc? What functions does each of these people or companies perform in the chain?
2. To what extent do they compete with each other? And with other supply chains?

Service providers

3. Are there any important services provided by other businesses that support or make this market chain viable? (*e.g. suppliers, transport services, storage facilities, communications, financial services*)
4. Are there any important services or infrastructure provided by government / local authorities that support or make this market chain viable? (*e.g. credit facilities, power and water*)

Business environment / institutions

5. What laws, formal rules, or regulations have a big influence (positive or negative) on the way in which this supply chain works?
6. Are there any informal customs, habits, and practices that shape the relationships (e.g. build trust) between market actors? (*e.g. customs about whom to sell to or buy from*)

Baseline performance of the market system

7. How many people do you employ normally at this time of year? Does it change seasonally? Where do your workers come from? Percentage of men / women?
8. How much do your workers normally earn? Do they receive other benefits?
9. Do profits change during the year (i.e. seasonally)? At what time of year do you employ the greatest / least number of people? In a normal year, how many staff would be working for you, and what would your profits be?
10. Who normally buys your products or uses your services – rich people, middle-class people, poor people? Could you estimate how much each of these households would typically consume per week?

Is this market usually competitive and well integrated?

11. Do you have competitors? Do you or your competitors control the supply and thus set the price of goods/services? If so, how do you / they establish and maintain this control?
12. Does the pattern of seasonal price variations in your area (affected by disaster) tend to be the same as the pattern in other regions or in the capital (after accounting for transport costs)? If not, why do you think seasonal price variations in this area are different from elsewhere?

Emergency-affected situation

How has the emergency affected the functioning of the market?

13. What impacts / changes have there been to your ability to stay in business and employ staff?
14. Have any particular market actors or functions in the value chain been especially affected?
15. How has the emergency affected important services or public infrastructure mentioned above?
16. How much more costly is it to do business as a result of the emergency? Which business costs have increased (fuel, storage, goods, labour, etc.) and by how much? How are you dealing with the emergency?
17. How have you adapted your operations to overcome challenges caused by the emergency?
18. How have other actors in the market chain adapted? (*e.g. input suppliers, transporters, producers*)

How has the emergency affected competition?

19. Has the emergency changed competition within your sector? (*e.g. have some been more severely affected by the disaster than your company?*)
20. Do you think you or your competitors have enough leverage to restrict supply and drive up prices now?

How is the market performing now?

21. Have your sales increased or decreased? If so, why?
22. Have prices for this product / service increased, decreased, or stayed the same, compared with the normal trends for this time of year? Specify by how much.
23. Are certain groups of consumers now effectively unable to purchase these goods / services because of high prices or lack of access to suppliers?

What if the purchasing power of your buyers was restored and you could continue to employ people?

24. If greater demand for your goods / services in the emergency zone could be guaranteed, to what extent would you be able to increase your supplies / business volumes in the affected area?
25. Are your employees still available, and are raw materials accessible now?
26. Which factors would be most likely to limit your capacity to increase volumes of business?

4.10 Data-collection sheets

Methods of recording the information gathered in interviews are discussed in Step 5. For many EMMA practitioners this is a personal choice. However, when it comes to quantitative data, it is a good idea to prepare standard data-collection sheets. These can help to ensure that data are captured systematically and in a consistent format so that they can be easily compared, aggregated, or utilized in a way that enables you to understand the market better.

You may find it useful to include a data table on the same sheet as the interview questions. These can be transposed, and calculations made and aggregated later in Step 6. Templates of these sheets can be found on EMMA reference manual CD-ROM.

Household income and expenditure data

A simple data sheet like that in Box 4.8 can be used to collect information about household income. A similar format is suitable for exploring how household expenditure is divided.

Box 4.8 Data-sheet for household income – example		
Major sources of income *including consumption of own food produce*	**Location** *Baseline situation*	**H/H size** *Emergency situation*
1. Consumption of own-grown maize	15 kg / week (est. value $6)	Nil (crop lost)
2. Profit from sales of own beans surplus	$75 lump sum (over 12 wks)	Nil (crop lost)
3. Wages for casual work in fish ponds	$8 / week	$4 / week
4. Remittances from brother in capital	$2 / week	$4 / week
5. Loan (advance) from landlord (i.e. 10 wks)	$50 sum until July	Nil (landlord displaced)
6. Government cash-for-work programme	Nil	$10 / week
Approximate total	*$27 / week*	*$18 / week*

Gap-analysis data

The datasheet illustrated in Box 4.9 is a useful way to summarize the analysis of the 'gap' (deficit) that a particular household is facing while awaiting the next harvest in ten weeks. The household has cut staple maize consumption from 15 to 8 kg per week as a coping strategy. But it faces a gap in household stocks of approximately 100 kg – or 10 kg per week for ten weeks.

Box 4.9 Data sheet for 'gaps' information – example

	Baseline situation	Emergency situation	Expected gap in next few weeks
Example A: Maize (staple food)			
Household consumption	15 kg/week	8 kg/week	10 kg/week for food, for next 10 wks 50 kg seed-corn by May
Household stocks	150 kg food (= 10 wks) 50 kg for seed-corn	50 kg (= 3 wks) No seed-corn	
Example B: Coastal fisheries (casual labour)			
Household income	$8/week	$4/week (work available but no transport to coast)	$15 for bus fares
Example C: Informal finance			
Household income	$50 lump sum (April) loan from landlord	Nil (Landlord displaced)	$5 /week for 10 weeks (for farm inputs, food)

Small traders / retailers data (in a supply market system)

The data sheet in Box 4.10 is a useful way to summarize the impact of the emergency on a small trader or local retailer. Remember that understanding the trend is just as important as getting precise figures.

Box 4.10 Data sheet for local trader / retailer – example

Type of actor: *village shop*		**Item:** *Beans (retail)*	**Location:** *Dhaizpur*
	Baseline	Emergency	Change or trend
Sales volume Kg / week	150–200	Oct: 200–300 Nov: 50–100	Sales peaked after quake, but now ~ 30% normal
Input costs $ / kg	25–30 wholesale + 6 for transport	Oct: 70 Nov: 50	Costs initially doubled but now returning to normal
Selling price $ / kg	40–45	Oct : 90 Nov: 55	Profit margins cut to minimum
Stocks held kg	1,200	300	Stocks very low for time of year

Producer data (in a supply market system)

A similar data sheet (Box 4.11) is useful for summarizing the experiences of local producers or farmers.

Box 4.11 Data sheet for local farmer / producer			
Type of actor	**Item**		**Location**
	Baseline	*Emergency*	*Change or trend*
Production Kg / month			
Sales $ / month			
Input costs $ / Kg			
Net earnings $ / month			

Employer data (in an income market system)

The kind of data sheet used for producers or retailers can also be adapted to employers in income market systems (Box 4.12).

Box 4.12 Data sheet for local employer – example			
Type of actor	**Employment activity**		**Location**
Fishing-boat owner	*In-shore fishing*		*Fezeen*
	Baseline situation	*Emergency situation*	*Change or trend*
Employment	36 man days/week (6 people) Had two of 13 boats in the local estuary (= 15%)	10 days/week (5 days x 2 people)	Lost one boat, and some crew displaced
Wages rate	1.50–2.00 typically	2.20–2.60	Wages have risen due to unavailability or loss of crew
Wage bill	$60/wk	$25/wk	
Sales	Would not disclose in detail	Would not disclose in detail	Sales have dropped by more than half

Checklist for Step 4

o   Interview agenda for gap analysis

o   Interview agenda for market-system analysis

o   Interview agenda for response analysis

o   Cash-feasibility agenda

o   Preparation of data sheets

STEP 5

Fieldwork activities and interviews

Cycling home with cut grass to be used as animal fodder, Cambodia

5.
Fieldwork
activities

Step 5 covers the EMMA fieldwork: interviews and other information gathering which make up the heart of the EMMA investigation. It includes advice on setting up and conducting interviews with different categories of informant: households, market actors, officials.

Before starting Step 5, you will have...

o   determined the key analytical questions that EMMA is trying to answer;
o   decided your fieldwork itinerary, and organised transport and accommodation;
o   prepared agendas (questions and interview structures) for different categories of informant;
o   designed data-collection and response forms to assist the fieldwork;
o   rehearsed your interview methods and techniques.

5.1 Overview of Step 5

Objectives

Gap analysis

- Confirm and if possible quantify high-priority un-met needs of various target groups.
- Verify your understanding of households' livelihood strategies and seasonal factors.
- Expose constraints on women's and men's access to and use of markets.

Market analysis

- Understand market-system structure, its conduct and performance prior to the crisis.
- Assess the effect of the crisis on the market system's infrastructure and supporting services.
- Understand the impact on different market actors and their coping strategies.
- Gather data about production and trade volumes, prices, and availability in the baseline and emergency-affected situations.
- Identify existing and expected constraints on the system's performance in the near future.

Response analysis

- Understand different target groups' preferred forms of assistance.
- Identify possible support actions that might strengthen market actors' coping strategies and encourage market-system recovery or better performance.

Activities

- Interviews with larger market actors (wholesalers, importers, processors) in the market system
- Interviews with knowledgeable key informants (government officials, development-agency staff, economic consultants, bank officers)
- Interviews / discussions with a sample of women and men from target-group households
- Interviews / discussions with a selection of local market actors (producers, retailers, traders, employers) in the crisis-affected area
- Informal and impromptu information gathering (walk-through meetings and road-side conversations)
- Daily revisions of the fieldwork agenda, interview questions, and information priorities, based on review and interpretation of the latest information gathered by the EMMA team

Key outputs

The outputs of this step will be recorded in three formats:

1. *Data sheets* – forms that systematically record quantitative data, for example:
    *   estimates of the scale of target households' priority gaps (un-met needs);
    *   estimates of baseline and current production, stocks, and trade volumes;
    *   data on baseline and current prices at key points in the market system.
2. *Interview records* – notes taken during interviews and meetings, for example:
    *   descriptions of livelihoods and coping strategies of various target groups;
    *   women's and men's preferences for various forms of humanitarian assistance;
    *   opinions about impacts of the crisis on people's businesses and the wider market system;
    *   information about regulation and market-actor conduct – cartels and market power;
    *   coping strategies reported as used by a range of market actors in reaction to the crisis;
    *   bottlenecks and constraints reported or anticipated by traders.
3. *Other field notes* – EMMA team members' own insights and interpretations during fieldwork:
    *   information about baseline market structure – including who is linked to whom;
    *   diagrams or sketches of the market system, or of household income and expenditure profiles;
    *   notes and observations for construction of seasonal calendars;
    *   factors affecting different target groups' access to the market system;
    *   views about the most urgent and effective possible forms of market-system support.

5.2 The fieldwork itinerary

Where, when, and with whom you conduct interviews will depend on many factors: on the geography of the market system; the time you have available; the locations of different market actors; and access constraints that the EMMA team face, due to security considerations, for example. What follows is merely a guide.

There are generally three investigative *arenas* for EMMA fieldwork in emergency situations.

1. *The emergency zone or crisis-affected area*
    This is where target households are located, along with local market actors (producers, retailers, traders, employers).

2. *Market-system hubs or trading centres*
    These are major towns, ports, or cities where larger market actors (importers, wholesalers, processing factories) are located.
3. *The government administrative centre*
    This is the closest major regional town or city where government officials, humanitarian agencies, and donor-agency headquarters are based, and other key informants are often found.

    You need to divide the team's time flexibly between these arenas. With luck, the second and third arenas will coincide. In practice your itinerary will often be dictated by transport logistics, timing, and field-access constraints.

First phase of fieldwork

*   Initial general interviews with larger market actors (wholesalers, importers, buyers)
*   Interviews with key informants (government officials, sector specialists, local NGO managers)

EMMA teams should begin fieldwork in the market system hub(s), and the administrative centre if different. Talk to larger market actors (e.g. wholesalers) who have an overview of the market system as a whole; take account of the role of services (such as finance, transport), policy, and regulation.

During this first phase, you should also interview any key informants who can help EMMA teams to build quickly on the preliminary understanding of the market system and the emergency situation established in Steps 1 and 3; for example, government officials, local NGO managers, and sector specialists.

The main mode of investigation in this phase is structured interviews. Initially, the information agendas (e.g. section 4.4) will be rather broad, but they should be adapted to suit the individual interviewed. Remember also to use early interviews to ask about other contacts: find out who the other main market actors are, and where they are located.

Two or three days of investigation in these arenas, often outside the emergency zone, make excellent preparation for fieldwork in the crisis-affected area. After interviewing a few knowledgeable informants and market actors, EMMA teams should expect to return to Steps 3 and 4 to revise their key analytical questions and preliminary maps.

Note: returning to previous steps is a normal part of the EMMA process. Understanding of the market system and the critical issues builds up gradually and iteratively. EMMA teams need to reflect regularly on the information received from interviews (e.g. on a daily basis), and use their reflections to refine their lines of enquiry in subsequent meetings.

Second phase of fieldwork

- Interviews with women and men in affected target-group households
- Meetings (and group discussions) with local market actors (traders, shop-keepers, producers)
- Informal roadside conversations and walk-through exercises

Fieldwork in the emergency zone is usually the most time-consuming phase, because of the numbers of people to be interviewed, and the logistics of travel. This is where a large EMMA field team can help – provided that each member is well oriented. The work involves interviews with a sample of women and men from different target groups, and meetings with local market actors (producers, retailers, traders, employers).

In general, it is best in any location to start by meeting local key informants – village elders, local government officials. This will avoid offending local norms and often leads to introductions to other important contacts. Then speak next to women and men in target households in the affected area – preferably separately. Afterwards, talk to the local market actors (producers, retailers, traders, buyers) with whom the target households say they come into contact, e.g. at local market places. A mixture of informal 'walk-through' conversations and more formal interviews is often advantageous.

There are advantages also in moving between different types of interview in different locations, so that varied perspectives enrich your understanding of the situation which you bring to later interviews.

After talking to small local actors, EMMA teams may find it useful to work back along the value chain or supply chain – following the links towards the larger market actors in the major trading centres and cities. This ensures that you focus efforts only on the market actors that are most relevant to the target population (see Box 3.6 about 'optimal ignorance').

Third phase of fieldwork

- Follow-up interviews with larger market actors
- Follow-up interviews with key informants

After fieldwork in the emergency area, it is very common to find that further detailed questions and more specific issues will have arisen. These may require more information from larger market actors and key informants. For example, EMMA teams may need to explore the feasibility of specific activities that are emerging as strong candidates for response options (section 9.7). Follow-up interviews will usually be needed with key informants in the trading hubs or administrative centres.

On-the-job analysis

By now, you should have realized that analysis of the information and data collected in the field needs to be initiated during the course of the fieldwork. In other words, Steps 6, 7, and 8 ideally begin during the fieldwork. After every interview, and at the end of each day, make time to ask: 'What does this information tell us about the key analytical questions that we are trying to answer?'

This thinking and reflection time is essential, and it is far more productive to reflect immediately when information is fresh, than wait until you are back at headquarters. Ideally, on a daily basis, teams need to...

- modify or re-draft market maps to reflect their evolving understanding of the system;
- check that the interview questions are still relevant. Modify them as necessary to reflect the most important gaps in your knowledge of the market system as the fieldwork progresses.

Be aware that as you gather and process information daily, you will probably add new interviews to your agenda and need to adjust plans and prioritize accordingly.

Box 5.1 Daily checklist during fieldwork

1. Update the baseline and emergency maps.
2. Update the seasonal calendars.
3. Summarise key findings from interviews / observations.
4. Complete / clarify your data sheets.
5. Review and revise your interview schedule.
6. Revise interview questionnaires / prompt sheets.

5.3 Allocating available interview time

There is never sufficient time to follow every lead, or speak to every person, so prioritization is essential. Work out how many 'interview hours' you are likely to be able to fit into the time you have available. This will depend on the number of days, travelling times, and the size of the EMMA team – i.e. how many interview pairs you can divide yourselves up into.

As a rough guide, you should allocate your available interview time (excluding travel time) in the proportions indicated in Box 5.2.

Box 5.2 Dividing up your interview time

Interview type	Share of time	Example
Target-population households	**15%**	*8 hours* *(12 short interviews)*
Local retailers, traders, buyers, or employers	**30%**	*12 hours* *(15 medium interviews)*
Traders, wholesalers, major buyers, importers in trading centres, city	**30%**	*12 hours* *(15 medium interviews)*
Other key Informants, officials, etc.	**15%**	*6 hours* *(6 long interviews)*
Contingency and follow-up interviews	**10%**	4 hours

It is vital to keep some time available for follow-up interviews. As your understanding of the market system grows and you begin to consider the response analysis, you may well need this time to return to explore particular issues or response opportunities in more detail.

5.4 Selecting whom to interview

Try and talk to as wide a range of people as time allows during EMMA fieldwork. Remember, however, that the EMMA process does not allow time for rigorous systematic surveying of households or market actors. At best, you will do well to speak to a small but roughly representative sample of women and men.

Box 5.3 Appropriate imprecision

EMMA cannot achieve the same sort of statistical accuracy as large surveys with dozens or hundreds of interviews. For example, suppose 20 people tell you how much they spend on rice each month. Their answers (averaged) will represent the wider population with only limited accuracy – perhaps plus or minus 10 per cent, at best.

Therefore, it is misleading to state the result like this: 'average spend = Rs 72.30'. It is too precise. A more correct finding would be 'average spend is in the range Rs 60–80'. If the sample is smaller (e.g. 10 people), the precision of findings will be even less: perhaps only plus or minus 30 per cent.

The best that EMMA can hope to achieve is a level of 'appropriate imprecision'. Instead of large samples, assume that findings are only very approximate, and try to cross-check (triangulate) them against other sources of information. The implications of this are clear in EMMA:

*   Do not waste time trying to get very precise answers to quantitative questions.
*   Do not use misleadingly precise results in your analysis.

Interviews with larger traders, employers, and buyers

Aim to interview the major market actors in the market system who are outside the local affected area. This may include larger traders, wholesalers and importers, in the major trading centres and cities. It may also involve service providers (from transport and finance sectors, for example).

Remember that traders, like everyone else, may have their own agenda and their own reason for wanting to talk to you. In general, there is probably little to be gained by group meetings of larger traders, and individual interviews are usually much easier to arrange.

You will identify who these people are through various networks, including the following:

- logistics officers of humanitarian agencies and NGOS, who sometimes have data bases of major suppliers;
- government officials and other key informants, who may know who the main players are;
- local traders, retailers, employers, who may direct you to their suppliers and buyers.

Remember: when a major emergency response is likely or expected, traders may have a very large stake in the outcomes of EMMA. For example, they may claim to have supply capacity because they hope to get orders. EMMA teams need to reflect on what they are told. Do not assume that anyone can actually deliver on what they tell you, unless they have signed a binding contract. There is no substitute for using your best judgement and common sense.

Key informants

Aim to interview any key individuals who are likely to understand the market system well, even though they are not trading in it themselves. They may include the following:

- officials in the local offices of Ministry of Agriculture, Livestock, etc.;
- staff of major UN and humanitarian agencies, e.g. FAO, WFP, UNDP, etc.;
- market or trading authorities in trading centres; officials in Customs offices (near borders);
- local NGO development-agency staff, including your own colleagues.

Often it will be necessary to introduce yourself to local elders or officials to get permission to make enquiries in the area. This can be a good opportunity to investigate their knowledge of the situation. Remember it is not only these people's knowledge that is valuable, but also their access to other information – reports and studies. For example, localized market studies (i.e. relating to the emergency zone) may be available from district government offices or local NGOs. Some government agencies, World Bank staff, or NGOs may have completed sub-sector analyses for specific markets.

National baseline price and volume data for various commodities and other products may be available from governments (e.g. a Consumer Price Index), or other agencies such as WFP, FAO FEWSNET, USAID, and other NGOs.

In food systems and other agriculture-related market systems especially, you may be able to access national-level information on markets and food security from WFP market profiles, CFSVA and CFSAM reports, and data from FEWSNET and FAOSTAT and USAID Bellmon Analyses (see web links in Boxes 1.1 and 1.2).

Household interviews

Aim to speak to a small but representative sample of women and men in target-group households. Do not neglect your agency's own staff: drivers, cleaners, and guards can be very useful sources of information. Ensure that your 'sample' includes, if relevant, households from different target groups:

- women and men from different locations, ethnic groups, etc.;
- households that represent groups with different livelihood strategies – farmers, wage labourers, fisher-folk, pastoralists, etc.;
- individuals representing different kinds of family structure – female-headed and male-headed, young, elderly, etc.

Ideally, interview women and men separately, representing up to five households from each type of target group, but this will depend on the diversity and complexity of the situation. Think about the timing and location of interviews or meetings. Women and men often have different daily timetables of responsibilities – for example, collecting water and firewood, seeking daily labour – which will affect whom you get to see and where it is best to meet them.

Remember: a small number of household interviews do not create a reliable picture on their own. Try to 'triangulate' (i.e. confirm) your findings by using at least two different information sources.

There are various ways to investigate information from households, and formal individual interviews are only one. Consider also more informal exercises such as 'walk-through' research in camps for refugees and displaced people – where discreet and brief conversations are held with random individuals as you wander around people's living areas. Although the information agenda (section 4.3) in such exercises may be restricted, this can be an efficient way to get a feel for the issues, needs, and preferences of a target population.

A slightly more formal investigation can often be done through focused group discussions, which can be a good way to hear lots of opinions quickly and spark new ideas (e.g. for response options). See the EMMA reference manual for further guidance on how to run focus groups.

Local market-actor interviews

Aim to interview a diverse sample of local retailers, buyers, traders, small-scale employers, etc., depending on their relevance to the market system and your EMMA objectives. Concentrate on the people or businesses that are most significant in the local economy and to the critical market system particularly.

It may be easier to have an informal discussion with several smaller market traders at an open market. In fact, trying to restrict the discussion to just one trader would be more difficult. In situations where there are too many local 'players' to interview all of them, you should adapt your sample to focus on those who are reported to be the most economically important.

- Householders, wage earners, and producers (farmers) should be able to point you to the most important local people to talk to.
- Retailers and traders will identify others: their suppliers and their competitors.
- Local agency staff / colleagues – including drivers and security guards – will often give you a good explanation of how the local economy works, if you ask them.

Expect local market actors to be busy people whose time is valuable. They may justifiably be suspicious or frightened of strangers asking questions about their business. The key to successful interviewing is to build a rapport and gain their trust. Act with modesty and gratitude towards them, and do not waste their time with unnecessary or intrusive details.

Box 5.4 Tips on interviewing local market traders

Timing: Interview at an appropriate, quiet time of the day, e.g. early morning as a shop opens, or after lunch. Get some advice on when is the best time to visit. Limit the interview to a maximum of 30 minutes, especially if you turn up at a busy time of day.

Avoid raising expectations: Do not be tempted to reinforce people's natural expectations that you are there to provide immediate assistance. Make it clear that EMMA is about assessment and planning. Make no promises of assistance at this stage.

Use maps and diagrams: Go prepared with a preliminary market-system map and seasonal calendar. Be ready to draw graphs to illustrate high- and low-season prices, for example. Update these diagrams together with traders, if they respond well to visual images. Encouraging informants to draw their own maps is a good way to get a more engaged response from interviewees, often revealing unexpected information that you might not have otherwise have looked for.

Sensitive Information: Respect interviewees' privacy. Some information that you need is commercially sensitive (e.g. sales, profits), so do not expect answers to direct questions. Use oblique approaches: 'What would a shop of about this size sell per week?' Do not demand people's names.

As well as formal individual interviews with local market actors, EMMA teams may learn much from brief and informal *'roadside'* conversations. These conversations – with randomly encountered individuals working in the market chain, such as producers or vendors – may last only five or ten minutes. As with *'walk-through'* exercises with households, the range of questions that you can ask may be limited, but it can still be an effective way to get a feel for the emergency situation and its impact on the local economy.

5.5 General advice on conducting interviews

Be clear and realistic about your EMMA objectives: before every interview, remind yourself of the key analytical questions to which you hope to find answers, and identify which topics are most relevant to this specific interview. Be brutally realistic about how much you can find out in the time available, e.g. 30 or 40 minutes.

Avoid duplication and interviewee-fatigue: be sure to co-ordinate with other NGOs operating in the emergency area to avoid duplicating interviews with the same traders using slightly different, yet related questionnaires. UN-OCHA often co-ordinates these activities.

Team organisation: use your team carefully. Have one person to ask questions and a second person to record responses in notes or on data sheets. Other team members can chat to and distract bystanders if necessary. The questioner should not write while interviewing. As in any normal conversation, she or he must maintain continual eye-contact, and demonstrate interest and appreciation of the interviewee's answers. If a translator is used, he or she should be introduced, but the questioner must still speak directly to the interviewee throughout the conversation. Review interview notes with translator after each interview.

Introduce yourself and your agency properly: explain clearly your purpose at the start of the interview. You want to plan effective humanitarian programmes to help people of the area, without harming market activity, i.e. you are not there to check licences or for tax purposes. For example: 'We are a study group from <your organisation>. We are looking at how communities affected by the crisis can get access to <critical product or items>. We want your help to understand the market for this product. We do not need to know your name, but please could you help us with some information?'

Think 'structured conversation' rather than 'survey': try to make the interview like a natural conversation, covering a few interesting topics. Do not make the interviewee think that you are only there to fill in a questionnaire. Let informants lead the conversation. Do not worry if you cannot cover every question in every interview.

Use open-ended and non-leading questions: in general, questions that encourage people to reflect and reveal details are best. Be a good listener. Avoid 'closed questions' that prompt simple Yes/No responses. And avoid 'leading questions' that simply invite people to confirm your own assumptions.

Be flexible and spontaneous: do not be constrained by your questionnaire. If you see or hear about something really interesting – if a delivery of new stock arrives, for example – follow your nose and ask about it. If you cannot get the information that you need directly, try other angles. For example: if a retailer cannot give estimated sales figures, ask them instead how many customers they see in a day, and how much a typical customer spends.

Do not be distracted: keep your key analytical questions in mind constantly, and do not waste your own or your interviewee's time going into unnecessary detail or exploring irrelevant lines of enquiry (see Box 3.6). For example, if you want to know the volume of trade in a particular location, you need estimates of actual sales from different traders. But if you only want to compare trade now with trade before the crisis, it is only the trend that matters (up a third, down a half, etc.), not actual sales figures.

5.6 Recording your findings

The most important task and difficult skill in interviewing is to record findings efficiently, so that you can use the information effectively later in analysis.

Taking interview notes

- Take brief notes of key points in the meeting, rather than attempt to record everything that is said. Focus on information that is most relevant to the EMMA objectives (key questions).
- Physically organize your notes around the main topics of the interview as you proceed: for example, keep separate pages in your notebook for different issues.
- Read, check, and discuss any ambiguity in your notes with other team members, immediately after each interview.

Recording data

- Quantitative data need to be recorded systematically on a data sheet. Data sheets must be prepared in advance (see Step 4), tailored to the interview questions and type of informant.
- Local traders, producers, and households may often use traditional or non-standard units for weights and measures. Find out and record the conversion factors. Record what interviewees say, but convert this to standard units as soon as possible.
- Do not get bogged down in unnecessary detail – estimates and approximations are good enough. If people cannot or will not give you figures, you may still be able to record the direction or pace of any changes.

In Step 4, various pro-forma data sheets are provided as examples. These data sheets will not fit every situation: they need to be tailored to suit the particular market system and the specific type of market actor whom you are planning to interview.

Using diagrams

Often it is useful to draw a diagram during the interview to represent (and check your understanding of) information given. For example, the relative importance to a trader of different business linkages might be represented by a diagram like the one in Box 5.5. This kind of information is easily incorporated later into a market-system map.

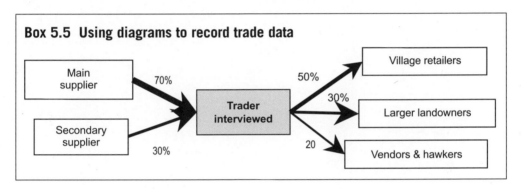

Box 5.5 Using diagrams to record trade data

Similarly, you can record information about other factors (e.g. seasonal issues) in simple diagrams which you later incorporate into your analysis, such as a seasonal calendar. See Box 5.6.

Box 5.6 Using diagrams for seasonal information

Employers	M	J	J	A	S	O	N	D	J	F	M	A
Price variations		Low					High	Peak				
Stock levels	High							Low				
Supply constraints					Roads flooded							
Labour availability			Low: planting							Low: harvesting		

5.
Fieldwork
activities

Field notes

Field notes are general observations and other information about the impacts of a crisis on actors, linkages, and market integration that may not be captured on your questionnaires and data sheets.

Observations: your eyes can tell you a lot, and it is important to note important trends, changes, or events in your target area. Noticing these trends and applying them to the current situation is key to adjusting yourself for upcoming interviews, analysing the changing situation, and preparing possible interventions that are relevant and timely.

- Does this economy (the target area) appear healthy?
- Do shops and transporters appear to be opening and active? Is the market area vibrant?
- Who is using the market – women, men, which target groups?
- Do you notice distributions or other interventions?
- Is the target community utilizing or finding alternatives to the critical market system (income and supply markets)?
- Are certain livelihoods groups or ethnicities excluded from the recovery process?

Checklist for Step 5

o   Conduct interviews with target groups, women, and men.

o   Conduct interviews with local traders and producers.

o   Conduct interviews with employers, key informants, other larger market actors.

o   Update the baseline and emergency maps and seasonal calendars.

o   Summarize key findings from interviews, observations, notes.

STEP 6
Mapping the market system

Carrying a fish to market in Kenya, during the East Africa food crisis.

Step 6 brings together the raw quantitative data and qualitative information collected during fieldwork in order to construct a concise and coherent description of the market system. The emphasis is on producing final versions of market maps, seasonal calendars, and household profiles that will inform the 'analytical' steps that follow.

Before starting Step 6, you will have...

o   prepared preliminary maps of the baseline and emergency-affected situations;

o   gathered information about how the market system performed before the crisis;

o   explored how the crisis has affected the market system, and how market actors are coping;

o   consulted market actors and key informants on possible market-support actions.

6.1 Overview of Step 6

Objectives

* Produce final versions of market maps, comparing baseline and emergency-affected situations.
* Produce final versions of seasonal calendars and household economic profiles for target groups.
* Write summary explanations of all market-system features that are relevant to the *key analytical questions* defined in Step 3.

Activities

* Sort and bring together information from your quantitative data sheets.
* Compile all the qualitative information in interview records and field notes.
* Re-draw final versions of both baseline and emergency market-system maps.
* Compile final versions of the market system's seasonal calendar.

Key outputs

* A final, seasonally adjusted, *baseline map* (or maps) representing the market system as it was before the onset of the emergency
* Data about numbers of market actors, prices, and volumes of production and trade in the baseline situation (shown either on the market map, or included in separate tables)
* Explanatory text describing the baseline market system's key features that are most relevant to the crisis-affected situation
* A final, seasonally adjusted, *emergency-affected map* (or maps), representing the market system as it is now
* Data about numbers of market actors, prices, stocks, and production and trade volumes in the emergency-affected situation (shown either on the market map, or in separate tables)
* Explanatory text describing the key aspects of the impact of the crisis on the market system, including major constraints, bottlenecks, and coping strategies of market actors
* A seasonal calendar for the market system

6.2 Baseline market-system map

The first main output from Step 6 is your final version of the *baseline market-system map*. Its purpose is to compare the 'normal' and 'crisis-affected' situations: it shows the market system *as it might have been now*, had the crisis not occurred. The final output will be a refined version of the preliminary baseline market map which you started in Step 3 and have been revising and developing during the course of the fieldwork.

The mapping process

To develop a final version of baseline market-system map, you will have to pull together, and represent, information from the many sources used during Steps 1–5, including background research (especially any previous market profiles or reports); interviews with key informants who had good sector knowledge, and with market-system actors, especially larger traders and businesses who were able to provide you with retrospective information.

The basic activities of market-system mapping were explained in Step 3:

- Start by getting a clear picture of the main structure of the market system (actors, pathways, and linkages), with the position or role of EMMA's target groups well defined.
- Add in the key inputs – providers, services, and infrastructure – especially those that have been most affected by the crisis. Indicate which actors or linkages are most dependent on these services.
- Add in the critical 'institutional' issues – again focusing attention on relevance to the crisis, and opportunities for humanitarian agencies to influence the situation.
- Incorporate 'quantitative' data – by adding in key numbers (section 6.4) or by using visual clues in the map (for example, different thicknesses of linkages).

Keep it simple

Market maps and calendars tend to start simple but become more complex during fieldwork, as interviews generate more information and data. By this stage your understanding of what is relevant and what is not should enable EMMA teams to focus only on the most relevant features of the map or calendar. You must refine and re-work complex diagrams, gradually simplifying them until you have a useful output.

In order to be effective as a communication device, the final market-system maps must be visually clear and simple, so that the key features stand out for the report reader and decision maker; and they must be seasonally relevant, showing the market system at the time of year when the emergency response is needed.

Remember, your main objective is to produce diagrams and an analysis that are direct and accessible to time-starved managers. This means being highly selective about the information that you eventually include and present: ruthlessly excluding superfluous information or data that are not relevant to the crisis situation and the humanitarian challenges. To achieve this state of 'optimal ignorance' (see Box 3.6), EMMA teams will inevitably end up having to discard some data that they worked hard to collect.

6.3 Emergency-affected market-system map

The second main output of Step 6 is a final version of the emergency-affected market-system map. The main purpose of the second map is to highlight how the market system's structure, capacity, and performance have been affected by the crisis. It is the core illustration, and your other descriptive texts and findings will be built around it.

A key aspect of mapping is comparison of the crisis-affected and baseline situations. This makes it easier to understand the current issues, problems, and opportunities. Marks or flags on the map draw attention to the important changes caused by the emergency, or arising from the humanitarian response.

The kinds of feature to highlight (with visual flags) on the emergency-affected map include the following:

- damage to assets or disruption to the livelihood activities of target households;
- partial or complete disruption of businesses (traders, retailers) in the supply / value chain;
- blockage or partial obstruction of particular linkages or relationships in the system;
- break-down or loss of key services or forms of infrastructure;
- emergence of temporary alternative pathways for items, e.g. via humanitarian activities;
- policies, regulations, or social norms that are acting as a constraint on the market system.

It is a good idea – for visual clarity and to focus readers' attention – to limit the number of flags on the map to a maximum of around ten. This means that you must focus on the priority issues: those that are having the greatest impact on the target population.

Explanatory text – map features

Maps do not tell the full story on their own. Both the baseline and emergency market-system maps should be backed up by short explanatory texts which draw attention to key features of the system that are *most relevant to the crisis-affected situation*.

This text will explain features of the system, such as the following:

- where (location on the map) and how (what activities and roles) different target groups are involved in the market system;
- which pathways (or chains) in the system are most important in meeting their needs;
- which market actors are the crucial important players in these chains;
- what forms of infrastructure and types of supporting service are especially important;
- any rules, regulations, social norms, or practices (conduct) that are significant factors affecting the performance of the system, or the access of particular target groups. This last point includes socially or culturally determined gender roles.

For every flag on the map, you will need to write a brief narrative text, explaining the nature of the impact or problem in descriptive terms. Keep your audience of busy decision makers in mind. Try to keep the text brief and relevant. See Box 6.1.

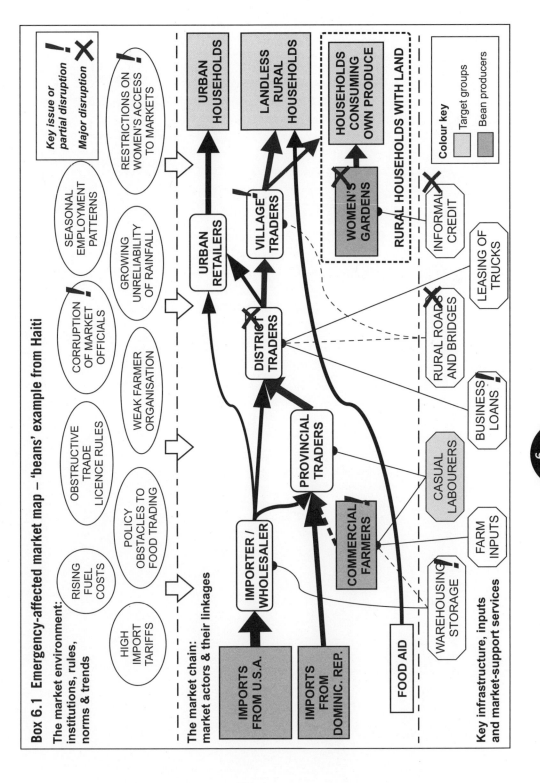

Box 6.1 Emergency-affected market map – 'beans' example from Haiti

The market environment:
institutions, rules, norms & trends

Key issue or partial disruption !
Major disruption ✗

- HIGH IMPORT TARIFFS
- RISING FUEL COSTS
- POLICY OBSTACLES TO FOOD TRADING
- OBSTRUCTIVE TRADE LICENCE RULES
- WEAK FARMER ORGANISATION
- CORRUPTION OF MARKET OFFICIALS !
- SEASONAL EMPLOYMENT PATTERNS
- GROWING UNRELIABILITY OF RAINFALL
- RESTRICTIONS ON WOMEN'S ACCESS TO MARKETS !

The market chain: market actors & their linkages

- IMPORTS FROM U.S.A.
- IMPORTS FROM DOMINIC. REP.
- FOOD AID
- IMPORTER / WHOLESALER
- COMMERCIAL FARMERS
- PROVINCIAL TRADERS
- DISTRICT TRADERS ✗
- URBAN RETAILERS
- VILLAGE TRADERS
- WOMEN'S GARDENS ✗
- URBAN HOUSEHOLDS
- LANDLESS RURAL HOUSEHOLDS
- HOUSEHOLDS CONSUMING OWN PRODUCE
- RURAL HOUSEHOLDS WITH LAND

Colour key
- Target groups
- Bean producers

Key infrastructure, inputs and market-support services

- WAREHOUSING STORAGE !
- FARM INPUTS
- CASUAL LABOURERS
- BUSINESS LOANS !
- RURAL ROADS AND BRIDGES ✗
- LEASING OF TRUCKS
- INFORMAL CREDIT ✗

6. Mapping the system

6.4 Quantification: putting numbers on the map

EMMA results will be more informative and compelling if you can rally some basic numbers to support your analysis and recommendations. This section explains how to make EMMA a quantitative, as well as descriptive, process.

The data that you compile here will be used later – in Step 8 especially. In particular, they will help you to draw conclusions about the capacity of the market system to play a role in humanitarian response: for example, by responding to local procurement activities, or reacting to increases in demand when cash-based assistance is given to target groups.

Two notes of caution

- It is often difficult and time-consuming to get accurate and reliable data about baseline market systems in a sudden-onset emergency situation. The results of quantitative analysis may not always justify the effort, skills, and time involved.
- Unless you have very solid evidence, assume that your data are imprecise and uncertain (see Box 5.3). If you interviewed only two or three traders, it would be better to give an approximate estimate (e.g. 100–150 tonnes) than to record an apparently accurate but actually very uncertain number (e.g. 137.5 tonnes).

Therefore, in practice, EMMA must compromise by focusing on only a few key pieces of data. Do not let the collection and analysis of quantitative data lead to neglect of more useful qualitative information.

The most useful quantitative data for EMMA to focus on are the following:

- *numbers* of market actors – at each step in the value / supply chain;
- *prices* of items – at key transaction points;
- *volumes* (quantities) – of goods or services produced and traded.

Box 6.2 Types of useful quantitative data in EMMA

Data	*Details*	*Why data are useful or important*
Actor numbers	Number of target households (differentiating between numbers of women and men if relevant) Number of market actors at key points in the chain	To understand scale of activities. To extrapolate from sample. To flag up risks of poor conduct (e.g. cartels).
Price data	Prices for target households, and at key points along supply / value chain	To help to diagnose supply or demand failure. To help to identify bottlenecks.
Volumes	Consumption or production by different target groups (differentiating between women and men if appropriate – e.g. for production) Trade volumes in local, provincial, national markets	To assess availability. To evaluate capacity to respond to procurement needs.

Numbers of market actors

It is important to look out for and take note of any significant changes in the numbers of market actors at key points in the system, especially if these changes point to the possibility of severe problems such as

- lack of physical access to the market system for any target groups;
- excessive concentration of market power in the hands of a few remaining actors (see 'competition' issues below);
- situations where there is a risk of cartels forming or monopolistic behaviour (poor conduct).

Disruption to the market system may involve the death or displacement of market actors and the destruction of their business assets, stocks, and premises. The number of market actors (including different target-group households), and their locations, can often be shown directly on the market-system map, as in Box 6.3.

Box 6.3 Showing actor numbers on market maps

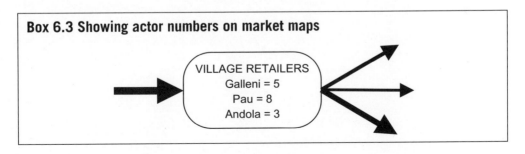

VILLAGE RETAILERS
Galleni = 5
Pau = 8
Andola = 3

Using price data

There is, at least in principle, a typical or average 'market' price associated with every transaction link in a supply chain or value chain at any time of year. It is especially useful to record changes in prices following the onset of an emergency. Comparison between baseline and crisis-affected prices – provided that they are seasonally relevant – can be useful for identifying bottlenecks or constraints in the market system caused by the crisis.

Price data can be shown on the map, as in Box 6.4.

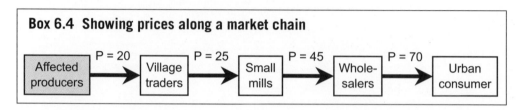

Box 6.4 Showing prices along a market chain

It is also useful to consider the direction and pace of price changes – also known as *price dynamics*. When it comes to assessing failures of supply and/or demand (in Step 8), knowing whether prices are generally rising, falling, or remaining stable is as important as knowing their relative level compared with the baseline situation.

Comparisons of prices prevailing at different times (i.e. baseline and current situations) need to take account of any *background inflation* – that is, general rises in prices in the national economy that are not related to the impact of the emergency. If background inflation is a significant factor (greater than 10 per cent p.a.), you should convert historical baseline prices into equivalent current prices. In situations of hyper-inflation or great instability of the local currency, it may be better to convert all prices into US dollars or Euros, using a realistic (informal or black-market) exchange rate.

Volumes of production and trade

Even though they are difficult to collect and analyse, data about the quantities, or volumes, of goods being produced and traded are potentially very valuable, for these reasons:

- In supply market systems, they are a guide to the availability of items, and the capacity of market actors to respond to the local procurement needs of both agencies and/or the target population.
- In income market systems, they can indicate the capacity of the market system to create income for the affected population by purchasing their produce, or their labour.
- Changes in volumes of production and trade are also important indicators of the general nature of the impact of the crisis on the market system (see the section on supply and demand failure in Step 8).

As a minimum, EMMA practitioners need to try to estimate (approximately) the seasonal production and trade volumes in the 'local economic area' where the affected population is located; and in the wider provincial or national economy within which the local area is embedded.

How to do it

There are essentially two ways of estimating the total production and trade in a given economic area (see Box 6.5). You can use whichever is easier, or if possible use both as a way to cross-check (triangulate) findings.

Method 1 – based on consumption

a. Estimate total consumption or usage in the economic area (using data about households).
b. Add any goods going out (exports) to other economic areas or markets (using data from traders).

Box 6.5 Estimating volumes from consumption data

Example of Method 1: consumption plus exports

Ghazia county has a population of approx 140,000 households.
Normally, in May–July, average household consumption = 2.5 kg lentils per month.
Estimated *baseline consumption* = 140,000 x 2.5 kg = 350 tonnes / month

At this time of year, Ghazia normally exports lentils to the capital city. Three main traders (who control two-thirds of the market) would normally export approximately 40 tonnes per month.
Estimated *baseline trade going out* of Ghazia = 40 ÷ 2/3 = 60 tonnes / month

Total production and trade (baseline) = 350 + 60 = 410 tonnes / month

---

Method 2 – based on production

a. Estimate total production in the economic area (using data from producers, government).

b. Add any goods coming in (imports) from other economic areas or markets (using data from traders).

It is important not to be intimidated by such calculations, nor to spend too much time on them. In an emergency situation, and especially with baseline data, the best you can realistically hope for is a very rough estimate of quantities: just a 'feel' for the scale of economic activity.

> ## Box 6.6 Estimating volumes from production data
>
> *Example of Method 2: production plus imports*
>
> Kandarpur district typically harvests approximately 12,000 tonnes of wheat in September /October, for consumption during the winter (six months).
> Estimated *production* = 12,000 ÷ 6 = 2,000 tonnes / month (spread over winter)
>
> During this season, the district also normally imports wheat from the southern region. The two main wholesalers (who jointly control 80 per cent of this market) typically bring in approximately 60 tonnes each week.
> Estimated *trade coming into* the district = 60 x 4 ÷ 80% = 300 tonnes / month
>
> Total production and trade (baseline) = 2,000 + 300 = 2,300 tonnes / month

Information about production and trade volumes can be included in the market-system map in two ways. If you only have very rough estimates, the relative importance of different linkages or pathways in the system can be illustrated by using different thicknesses of arrows. Alternatively, numerical estimates at key points in the system can be overlaid on the map, as in Box 6.8.

6.5 Availability (stocks and lead times)

As well as getting a sense of production and trade volumes in supply market systems, it will be very useful (in Step 9) to have information about availability. These data include the following:

- the stocks held by different types of market actor along a supply chain, and
- the lead-times (between order and delivery) expected at each link in the chain.

This information will come from the interviews with market actors (traders, retailers etc.). When investigating lead-times, treat people's responses cautiously. Traders may exaggerate how quickly they can obtain supplies, in order to impress you, or because they are unaware of bottlenecks elsewhere. Always check with other market actors in the chain.

Information about 'availability' can be usefully summarized in a table like Box 6.7.

Box 6.7 Analysis of availability along a supply chain

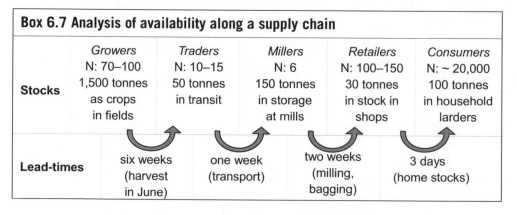

	Growers N: 70–100	Traders N: 10–15	Millers N: 6	Retailers N: 100–150	Consumers N: ~ 20,000
Stocks	1,500 tonnes as crops in fields	50 tonnes in transit	150 tonnes in storage at mills	30 tonnes in stock in shops	100 tonnes in household larders
Lead-times	six weeks (harvest in June)	one week (transport)	two weeks (milling, bagging)	3 days (home stocks)	

Box 6.8 Showing data about production and trade volumes on market maps – 'beans' example from Haiti

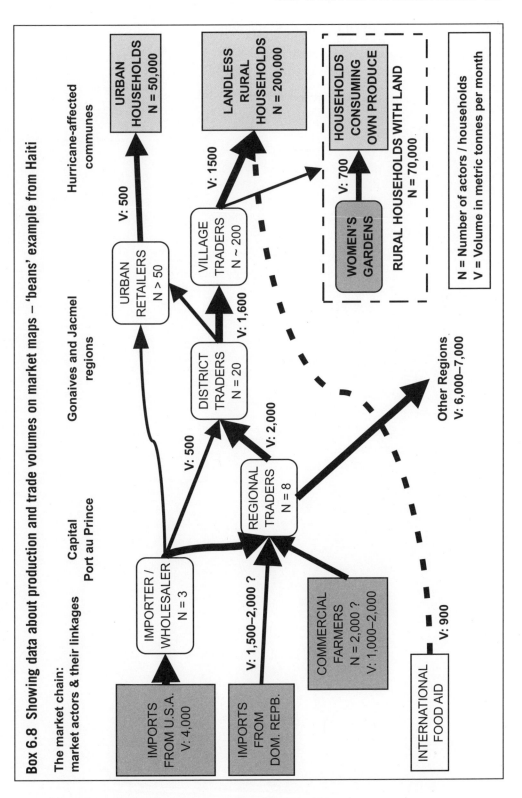

The market chain:
market actors & their linkages

Capital
Port au Prince

Gonaives and Jacmel
regions

Hurricane-affected
communes

URBAN
HOUSEHOLDS
N = 50,000

LANDLESS
RURAL
HOUSEHOLDS
N = 200,000

HOUSEHOLDS
CONSUMING
OWN PRODUCE

RURAL HOUSEHOLDS WITH LAND
N = 70,000

WOMEN'S
GARDENS

V: 700

V: 1500

V: 500

URBAN
RETAILERS
N > 50

VILLAGE
TRADERS
N ~ 200

V: 1,600

V: 500

DISTRICT
TRADERS
N = 20

V: 2,000

REGIONAL
TRADERS
N = 8

Other Regions
V: 6,000–7,000

IMPORTER /
WHOLESALER
N = 3

V: 1,500–2,000 ?

COMMERCIAL
FARMERS
N = 2,000 ?
V: 1,000–2,000

IMPORTS
FROM U.S.A.
V: 4,000

IMPORTS
FROM
DOM. REPB.

INTERNATIONAL
FOOD AID

V: 900

N = Number of actors / households
V = Volume in metric tonnes per month

6.
Mapping
the system

6.6 Seasonal calendar for a market system

Many market systems have strong seasonal variations in the patterns of production, trade, and prices. These patterns may reveal themselves through seasonal price fluctuations for inputs and outputs. Or they may involve major seasonal shifts of activity as people move, for example, between farming and wage employment.

This is most obvious in agricultural market systems – with shifts in demand for labour for ploughing, weeding, harvesting; and a surge in the supply of produce after harvesting. However, seasonal patterns may also feature in shelter-related markets, and in off-farm activities that are affected by weather or road access, for example. There is often a strong gender-related dimension to these patterns, as the roles and responsibilities of women and men differ. These need to be understood, since emergencies typically have different impacts on women's and men's time.

It is essential that EMMA users are able to distinguish 'normal' seasonal fluctuations in prices and trade volumes from the disruptions created by an emergency situation. Otherwise, your diagnosis of market-system problems and proposed solutions will be flawed. The baseline market map should represent a 'seasonally relevant' picture.

It is a good idea, therefore, to construct a simple seasonal calendar for each market system analysed, to capture the 'normal' seasonal patterns of price and trade. This can also be used to describe other important features of the system which may be relevant to the humanitarian response.

Box 6.9 Seasonal calendar for a market system – example

Market system (e.g. Beans)	S	O	N	D	J	F	M	A	M	J	J	A
Volume of trade			Low			High				Low		High
Prices at market				Peak $			Low $					Low $
Input purchases		$					$					
Road conditions	Floods											
Risk of crop pests			High						High			

Checklist for Step 6

o   Baseline and emergency-affected market maps finalized

o   Appropriate details quantified: actor numbers, prices, and availability

o   Key features of the system flagged up and described

o   Seasonal calendar finalized

STEP 7
Gap analysis

Photo credit: Geoff Sayer/Oxfam

Handing out mosquito nets in Bubulo village, Uganda

Step 7 completes the gap-analysis strand. It should produce a final estimate of the total shortfall or gap which the target population is facing for the critical item or service. This estimate will be needed by the EMMA team in Step 8 to assess whether, and to what extent, the critical market system is able to fill the gap.

Before starting Step 7, you will have...

o   investigated and confirmed the high-priority needs of households in each target group;
o   sketched outlines of household economic profiles and seasonal factors;
o   investigated any constraints on their access to the critical market system;
o   consulted target groups on their ideas and preferences for humanitarian assistance.

7.1 Overview of Step 7

Objectives

*   Calculate the magnitude of emergency response required, based on a good-enough estimate of the total gap that the target population is facing.
*   Analyse how important the gaps are within the economic profiles of different target groups, and factor in their preferences for the form of assistance offered.
*   Draw conclusions about any key factors influencing different target groups' *access* to the market system.

Activities

Compile data

*   Compile all available qualitative information about priority needs, preferences, and access constraints (from background research, emergency needs assessments, interview records, and field notes).
*   Sort and compile all quantitative data (from household surveys and interview data sheets).

Analysis and interpretation

*   Draw conclusions about target groups' priority needs, access constraints, and preferences.
*   Estimate the total gap that the target population faces.

Key outputs

*   A simple report table (e.g. Box 7.1) which summarizes the most essential details and characteristics of each of the target groups – their numbers, locations, income profile
*   A more detailed matrix (e.g. Box 7.2) which quantifies the priority needs for each target group, and shows the total gap estimated for the target population
*   Information about the likely duration of gaps, the access constraints, and the preferences expressed by different target groups about the form of assistance that they need
*   Notes to record the assumptions made in estimating these numbers, and highlighting any significant risks (e.g. a delay in expected assistance from another agency)

7.2 Target population: essential details

The first output is a final table summarizing general information about the target population: their numbers, location, and essential characteristics from an EMMA perspective. This table is a final version of Box 1.7, first drafted in Step 1, but with details enriched and confirmed by the household survey / interviews in Step 5.

This table will also answer the fundamental humanitarian questions:
- What is the geographic area in greatest need of assistance?
- Who are those who are most in need of assistance or most at risk?
- How many people are at risk and/or in need of assistance?

If the affected population was divided into target groups in the field work, this table will break down the information accordingly. The final EMMA report may also require a brief explanation of why separate target groups were chosen and defined in this way.

Box 7.1 Target-population details – example				
Target groups	*Female*	*Male*	*Location*	*Essential characteristics*
1. Rural landless households	42,000	35,000	~ 130 villages in the valleys south of Geld	Typically rely on seasonal work for maize farmers. Facing no income from agricultural work until at least March next year.
2. Rural subsistence small-holders	21,000	15,000		Typically rely on production of food staples (beans, cassava) for 40–60% of food needs. Most lost 90% of own crops and stored food.
3. Extra-vulnerable urban households	12,000	5,000	Geld, Madi and 3 small towns	Typically rely on occasional casual labour, charity, and remittances from relatives. Badly affected by rising food prices.
Total population	75,000	55,000		

7.3 Numerical gap analysis

The second task is to produce a gap analysis (Box 7.3) which sums up EMMA's best estimate of the total 'gaps' facing the target population. This finding will be used in Step 8 especially.

The nature of this 'gap' depends on the reason why the market system was selected as critical. See Box 7.2.

Box 7.2 Reasons why a market system might be critical	
Why system is critical	*Nature of gap*
It supplies food or items needed for ensuring survival	Shortfall between what households have and what is required to meet minimum standards for protecting life (c.f. Sphere)
It supplies inputs or assets for protecting livelihoods	Shortfall in inputs, assets, or services that households need to protect and sustain livelihood activities (e.g. food production)
It provides income, wages, or access to buyers	Loss of opportunity to sell labour, livestock, surplus produce, etc. which households need in order to earn a minimum essential income

The reasons may vary from one target group to another within the same market system. For example, the beans market system in Haiti (Box 6.1) was critical as a source of food for urban and landless rural households. But it was also critical as a source of income for many women producers on rural small-holdings.

Alongside numerical estimates, the gap-analysis table should include information about the following factors:

* *duration:* how long the specific gap is expected to last;
* *preferences:* target households' wishes about the form that assistance takes;
* *other assistance:* e.g. distributions from other agencies / government, or appeals in the pipeline.

Box 7.3 Summary of gap analysis – example						
Target group	*H-h in need*	*Household shortfall**	*Other aid*	*Total gap*	*Likely gap duration*	*Prefs for help*
Rural landless households	20,000	10 kg/week	–	200 tonnes per week	Thru to end of August	Mostly In-kind
Rural subsistence farmers	14,000	4 kg/week food needs (+$10/week lost income)	–	55 tonnes per week	Thru to end of June (next harvest)	Mostly cash
Vulnerable urban households	9,000	5 kg/week (due to high prices)	10 tons per week (Church)	35 tonnes per week	Until prices return to normal	Mostly cash
TOTAL	43,000			290 tonnes per week		

How to do this

- Draw upon existing emergency needs assessments, which may have detailed information on priority needs (especially for food and essential items).
- Collate your findings about household consumption, stocks, and shortfalls from the sample interviews with affected households.
- Use the seasonal calendar (see below) to inform the estimates of likely duration of shortfall (e.g. by considering seasonal patterns in prices and availability).
- Record any assumptions that you make about planned or actual assistance from other agencies.

UN cluster meetings (when well run) can play an important role in gap analysis – especially for high-priority items like food, shelter materials, and WASH items. They will often be the best source of information about the plans of all other agencies.

Minimum standards

For minimum nutritional dietary requirements, see Sphere standards and rations information in the WFP EFSA handbook (WFP 2009). The NutVal site (www.nutval. net) provides a spreadsheet application for planning and monitoring the nutritional content of general food-aid rations.

Estimates of shortfalls may need to take account of household stocks, including standing crops. See Box 7.4.

Box 7.4 Allowing for stocks in estimating gaps

Assume you find that normal household consumption is about 20 kg / week
And you find household stocks left after shock   = 70 kg
Plus expected harvest from damaged crops   = 200 kg
Total   = 270 kg
Length of time stocks at this time of year are normally expected to last = 30 weeks
Then SHORTFALL for next 30 weeks = 20 – (270 / 30) = 11 kg per week

---

For other minimum standards for meeting emergency needs, see Sphere standards. For minimum income requirements, the Household Economy Approach definitions are useful; see Box 7.5.

7.
Gap
analysis

> **Box 7.5 HEA definitions for essential income requirements**
>
> **The survival threshold** represents the total income required to cover:
> a) 100% of minimum food-energy needs (2,100 kcals per person), plus
> b) costs associated with food preparation and consumption (e.g. salt, soap, kerosene and/or firewood for cooking and basic lighting), plus
> c) any expenditure on water for human consumption.
>
> **The livelihoods-protection threshold** represents the total income required to sustain local livelihoods. This means total expenditure to:
> a) ensure basic survival (see above), plus
> b) maintain access to basic services (e.g. routine medical and schooling expenses), plus
> c) sustain livelihoods in the medium to longer term (e.g. regular purchases of seeds, fertilizer, veterinary drugs, etc.), plus
> d) achieve a minimum locally acceptable standard of living (e.g. purchase of basic clothing, coffee/tea).
>
> *Source:* FEG Consulting and Save the Children, 2008

7.4 Qualitative aspects of gap analysis

The numerical gap analysis is usually only part of the picture. It needs to be backed up by careful consideration of any significant qualitative issues and contexts identified during the fieldwork (Step 5), as follows.

Qualitative factors or contexts

- Constraints on women's and men's physical access to the market system
- Transport needs related to market access
- Ethnic, gender-related, or other social barriers to participation or access in the system
- Seasonal factors (other than duration of shortfall)
- Particular impacts that affect different target groups in different ways
- Particular coping strategies that are being used to meet this priority need
- Particular preferences or ideas about the response options
- Specific risks or problems that rule out any of the preliminary response options

These types of finding must be identified and recorded. They will often contribute ideas for response options in Step 9, and must influence the decisions and recommendations made at that point. Remember that diverse groups, especially women and men, experience the impact of emergencies differently. Their needs, preferences, and opportunities cannot be assumed to be the same.

> ### Box 7.6 Preferences for alternative forms of assistance
>
> In 2008, IRC conducted a study of the firewood market system in camps for internally displaced people in Pakistan's North-West Frontier Province, since obtaining fuel for cooking was a major problem and risk for women and children. An initial analytical issue was whether women would prefer cash or physical distributions of firewood. Women in the camps actually reported a preference for distributions of liquefied petroleum gas (LPG) for cooking. Adoption of LPG would save women's time – when they are already over-burdened with emergency-related responsibilities. It would also reduce local environmental damage and risks for children associated with scavenging for wood.

Qualitative factors are likely to be especially significant and powerful issues in conflict settings, and also in situations where different target groups have very distinct needs or perspectives.

How to do this

- Review interviews with key informants who are most knowledgeable about the emergency context.
- Review field notes from household interviews.
- Analyse a seasonal calendar for the different household target groups (see Box 7.7).
- Analyse changes in household economic profile (see Box 7.8) (income markets especially).

7.5 Household seasonal calendar

If seasonal factors are likely to be particularly important – for example in forming people's preferences or determining the duration of gaps – then a household-level calendar can be useful as a way of collating and summarizing information from household interviews. See Box 7.7.

7.
Gap
analysis

Box 7.7 Household seasonal calendar – example

Target group	S	O	N	D	J	F	M	A	M	J	J	A
Women's roles												
Income levels			Low				High					
Loan repayments				$		$					$	
Holiday / festivities				$					$			
School terms		Term A						Term B				
Shelter activities				Brick making				Thatch				
Men's roles												
Fodder availability									Low			
Livestock moves		Low ground					High ground					
Casual employment		$					$					

Remember to think about the different roles and responsibilities that are assumed by women and men within households. It may be valuable to separate these clearly in the seasonal calendar, so that differences in impacts and needs are clearly recognized.

7.6 Household income and expenditure profiles

The introductory chapter gives an overview of this tool in section 0.9. The main value of these profiles for EMMA comes from examination of changes in people's income or expenditure patterns as a result of the crisis. For further information, see FEG Consulting and Save the Children, 2008.

Detailed profiles of household income and expenditure (e.g. Boxes 0.16 and 0.17) may be especially valuable for EMMA exercises where medium-term or long-term (e.g. one-year or two-year) programmes towards economic recovery are envisaged. This is more likely in EMMA studies of income market systems. Do not wait until the emergency phase is over before starting this

If you have very little time, your priority should be to find out how the income or expenditure associated with the critical market system has changed. How have changes in income been accommodated by households in their consumption patterns? See Box 7.8.

Box 7.8 Changes to expenditure profile – example

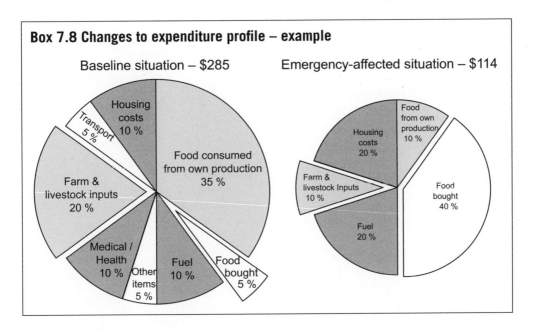

Baseline situation – $285   Emergency-affected situation – $114

Box 7.9 Simple analysis of changes in household income and expenditure

	Baseline		*Emergency*	
Total income (including self-consumed produce)	$30		$20	
Monthly income – agricultural labour	$20	65%	$5	25%
Monthly expenditure – beans	$10	30%	$15	75%

How to analyse income and expenditure profiles

- Remember to distinguish between income sources and financial responsibilities of women and men within households wherever possible.
- Look for trends and changes in relative proportions – in expenses, in incomes, in benefits.
- Look for basic capacity to meet needs (e.g. food basket).
- Look especially at the role of remittances and loans.
- Relate findings to the other qualitative results described above.
- Highlight long-term negative coping strategies (e.g. failure to feed or treat livestock, reduced agricultural inputs, withdrawing children from school).
- Look at unusual and striking findings (e.g. a high proportion of expenditure on particular items such as soap, sugar).

Checklist for Step 7

o   Essential details about target population

o   Summary of gap analysis (numerical data)

o   Qualitative issues and preferences of target groups

o   Seasonal calendar

o   Changes to households' income and expenditure profiles

STEP 8
Market-system analysis

A local water seller in Myanmar.

Step 8 completes the market-analysis strand, using the maps and calendars from Step 6 and the gap analysis from Step 7. This is one of the most crucial steps in EMMA. It involves a final assessment of the capacity of the critical market system, through increased production and trade, to fill the gaps facing the target population. This result forms a key input to the final response analysis in Step 9.

8.
Market-
system
analysis

Before starting Step 8, you will have...

o   explored how the crisis has affected actors in the system, and how they are responding;
o   consulted market actors and key informants on possible market-support actions;
o   completed the baseline and emergency-affected market maps;
o   drawn up a seasonal calendar for the market system;
o   completed the gap-analysis strand.

8.1 Overview of Step 8

Objectives

- Analyse *availability* and the principal supply and/or demand problems in the market system.
- Analyse and estimate the market system's existing or potential capacity to contribute to the required emergency response calculated in Step 7.
- Identify plausible options for indirect market-system support for consideration in Step 9.
- Answer, and draw conclusions about, the key analytical questions defined in Step 3.

Activities

Section 8.3: Baseline analysis

- Assessment of the market system's prior capacity and performance
- Analysis of data on volumes of production and trade, market integration, competition, and conduct

Section 8.4: Impact analysis

- Exploration of the impact of the emergency
- Comparisons of baseline and emergency situations in terms of trade volumes, prices, integration, and conduct

Sections 8.5–8.6: Future forecast

- Estimates of the market system's capacity to contribute to emergency response
- Identification of market-support options

Key outputs

- *How it was before:* an assessment of the market system's baseline capacity and performance
- *What has happened:* findings about the impact of the emergency on the market system; and in particular an analysis of supply-and-demand problems in the emergency-affected situation
- *How it is likely to perform in future:* an appraisal of the system's capacity and potential to contribute to the emergency response
- *Market-support options:* a list of possible emergency market-support options (to reinforce local capacity to contribute to humanitarian response), for consideration in Step 9

8.2 Outline of the analysis process

The essential aim of Step 8 is to assess whether the market system could contribute usefully and reliably to the emergency response. (See Box 8.1 for a definition.) If the answer is Yes, then Step 8 also aims to do the following:
*   estimate its capacity to contribute to meeting the gap, and
*   identify any support opportunities that could restore or increase this capacity.

Box 8.1 'Contributing to humanitarian response' – a definition

A market system is capable of contributing to the emergency response if, without causing harmful changes in prices or availability for others, it can provide:
*   a sufficient and reasonably priced supply of the critical food, items, or services directly to the target population – assuming that the latter has access and purchasing power (e.g. cash, vouchers);
*   a reliable and reasonably priced source of the critical food, items, or services for local procurement by humanitarian agencies; or
*   a reliable outlet (i.e. employers, buyers) and fair price for target populations' labour or produce – and thus a critical source of income.

In order to make this assessment, EMMA teams need to progress through a series of analytical stages, which are best represented by these four simple questions:
1. *Baseline:* what was the market system's capacity and performance before the emergency?
2. *Impacts:* what has happened to the market system in the emergency situation?
3. *Forecast:* how well is the system likely to contribute to emergency response in future?
4. *Support:* what options exist for restoring or strengthening the market system's capabilities?

Evidence

Step 8 brings together and uses the evidence – information and data – collected through background research and fieldwork, and the production of maps and seasonal calendars.

Box 8.2 Types of data and information used in market-system analysis	
Field observations	Observed disruptions to producers and businesses Reported disruptions to market linkages, transactions Reported disruptions to infrastructure and supporting services
Availability	Volumes of production and trade in different parts of system Current stocks and lead-times for supplies
Market integration	Strength of trade linkages with other, unaffected markets
Price information	Changes in prices compared with baseline situation Price trends (direction and volatility of price movements) Analysis of margins along the chain
Conduct of market actors	Actor numbers (and implications for market power) Uncompetitive behaviour or rules, cartels and barriers to entry

8.3 Baseline analysis

This element of the market analysis consists of three main questions:
- How did the baseline capacity compare with the challenge estimated by the gap analysis?
- How well integrated was the market system before the emergency?
- How much competition was there in the market system before the emergency?

Market-system capacity

With luck, enough data were collected (in Step 6) to make approximate numerical estimates of baseline economic activity (i.e. volumes of production and trade).
- In supply market systems, these data relate to the availability of items and capacity of market actors to respond to the procurement needs of humanitarian agencies or target population.
- In income market systems, they indicate the capacity of the market system to create earnings for the affected population by purchasing their produce or their labour.

It is important that these baseline estimates are seasonally relevant: i.e. they should offer a good basis for comparisons with the emergency-response requirements at this time of year.

These estimates should also be made, if possible at two or three different economic scales (see Box 8.3):
- within the local emergency-affected area (e.g. disaster zone);

- in the wider provincial / regional market (e.g. districts around a major trade hub);
- in the national market.

This enables EMMA to estimate the underlying 'normal' capacity of the market actors. By comparing this information with gap-analysis results, you will get an immediate feel for the scale of the emergency-response challenge facing the market system.

Box 8.3 Baseline production and trade volumes – example			
Volumes of production and trade (MT per month)	*National market*	*Provincial market*	*Local affected area*
Baseline activity	5,000	1,200	200
Gap facing the target population in the affected area = 350 (from Step 7)			

Market integration

Market integration is a measure of the degree to which market systems in different geographical areas are connected to each other. When markets are integrated, critical items or food stuffs will flow more easily from surplus areas to deficit areas; from producers to consumers; from ports and border crossings into more remote areas. When markets are fragmented, in contrast, it is difficult or expensive to move goods, and prices vary widely between locations and seasons.

The degree of market integration is a vital consideration for EMMA's analysis of appropriate responses.

- A local market system which was well integrated with wider markets in the baseline situation is much more likely to be able to expand trade to meet emergency needs.
- Where local markets are well integrated with larger markets, critical items, services, or food are more easily available and prices are more stable.
- Local procurement and cash-based interventions are highly dependent on market integration, which will enable critical items or food to flow from other surplus regions.
- Where local markets are fragmented – i.e. poorly integrated with larger markets – prices tend to be more volatile. Target groups will experience higher prices (lower income) more often.

How to assess market integration

If data are available, detailed price patterns over time usually indicate how well integrated markets are. See Box 8.4.

8.
Market-
system
analysis

In *strongly integrated markets*, high prices in deficit areas give traders an incentive to bring goods from surplus areas. Therefore

* prices tend to follow similar seasonal patterns, rising and falling in unison; and
* the price difference between markets stays relatively constant (represented by grey shading in the box).

In *weakly integrated (or fragmented) markets*, high prices in deficit areas do not create sufficient incentives for traders to move goods, due to high transaction costs (e.g. insecurity, washed-out roads). Therefore

* prices tend to follow dissimilar patterns; and
* big seasonal variations occur in the price difference between markets (grey shading in the box).

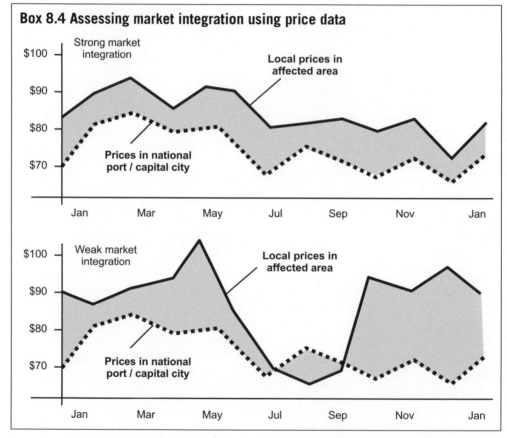

Box 8.4 Assessing market integration using price data

For more detailed guidance on market integration, consult the EMMA reference manual.

In the absence of detailed price-series data, it is usually possible to get a well-informed view of market integration from local and regional traders (Step 5). Interviews should reveal the following:

* where the main trade flows normally come from, or go to;
* what proportion of local production and trade is imported (or exported);

- whether local price peaks and troughs normally coincide with national ones;
- whether there are certain times of year when transport is restricted/difficult;
- whether there are other reasons why trade is restricted or markets segmented.

Box 8.5 Weak market integration – example from Haiti

EMMA analysis of the beans market system in Haiti in 2008 found that rural markets in different provinces were highly segmented (not integrated well).

This, it emerged, was because producers' access to their corresponding commodity markets in the capital Port au Prince was tightly controlled by regionally based trading clans, or cartels. After the hurricanes struck, these cartels had the effect of restricting the flow of food between different parts of the island.

Baseline competition and market power

EMMA teams must also try to assess conduct in the baseline market system, establishing how market actors did business with each other, and especially who set the prices in transactions. A market system that suffered from abuse of market power before a crisis is unlikely to perform better in an emergency.

Box 8.6 Competition and market power

Competition is about rivalry in the market place. Competition exists where buyers or sellers have a real choice between alternative market actors, based on who provides the cheapest or best goods, the highest wages, etc. The opposite of competition is market power, especially 'monopoly'. Market power arises when a single market actor – or a small cartel working in collusion – is able to dictate or strongly influence prices in their own favour, thus earning excess profits. As well as monopoly over trade, market power can stem from monopolistic control over resources, services, or knowledge.

Competition and market power form one dimension of conduct, but there are others (both positive and negative). EMMA teams need to note any significant forms of conduct in the baseline system which may undermine or support the performance of the market system in the emergency context. For further reading, see the FEWS NET market guide (FEWS NET, 2008).

Positive aspects of conduct may include the following:
- competition: households have a good choice of alternative suppliers (retailers, traders);
- embedded services: wholesalers and retailers offer credit or other services to their customers;

- risk management: businesses guarantee sales or advance loans to their suppliers (e.g. farmers);
- collective market power: small-scale farmers market their produce collectively.

Negative aspects of conduct could include:
- monopolistic behaviour: collusion by groups of traders (cartels) to influence prices in their favour;
- market distortion: prices are set by government in ways which disadvantage the vulnerable or depress economic activity;
- exclusion / barriers to entry: restrictions on where and when certain actors can trade.

8.4 Impacts of the emergency

This element of the analysis can be reduced to five main questions:
1.   What impacts on the market system have been observed in the emergency situation?
2.   How does the market system's current level of trade and availability compare with the baseline?
3.   Is the market system's performance essentially limited by supply problems, demand problems, or both?
4.   How has market integration been affected?
5.   How have competition and market power been affected?

Observations and mapping of emergency impacts

The major impacts of the emergency will have been observed by EMMA teams in the field; reported by market actors in their interviews (Step 5); and included in the market map of the emergency-affected situation (Step 6). Many different kinds of impact may have been reported, and it is important to focus attention on the parts of the system (and the impacts) that matter most to the target population. See Box 8.7.

The market maps can help with this focus, in two ways:
- by illustrating how different target groups interact or engage with the market system; and
- by conveying a sense of the relative economic scale of different actors, linkages, or pathways.

Box 8.7 Focus on the impacts that matter – an example of market segmentation

During EMMA fieldwork, wholesalers of rice, interviewed in a trading town, report that the major emergency impact (for them) has been the large-scale destruction of warehouse stocks.

However, market mapping shows that the wholesalers' produce mainly goes to export buyers, and is of a higher grade than the rice generally consumed by vulnerable target groups, who rely mostly on rice grown relatively locally by small-holder farmers; in other words, the market for rice is segmented.

The EMMA team therefore decide to concentrate attention on response options that address the production constraints faced by these small-scale farmers.

With this focus in mind, EMMA teams must do all of the following.

1. Review the market maps, interview findings, and field notes.
2. Identify the specific 'impacts' on the market system that are most significant for the target population, and relevant to their emergency needs (the gap), for example:
    *   reduced production or loss of previous stocks (e.g. food crops);
    *   loss of key actors in the supply chain/value chain that target groups use;
    *   damage to vital infrastructure, or disruption to key services;
    *   bottlenecks in transportation (e.g. roads, insecurity).
3. List any market-support ideas relating to these impacts that emerged during the EMMA process, e.g. solutions and support proposed by producers and traders (see section 8.6). These preliminary response options will form an input to Step 9.

Market-system capacity in an emergency situation

What changes have taken place in the volume of production and trade at different geographical scales, as a result of the emergency? Alongside price data, these changes are key indicators of the impact of the crisis on the market system. Comparing them with the baseline estimates above provides further insight into the magnitude of the impact on the market system. See Boxes 8.8 and 8.9.

It is important not to get stuck on detail with these estimates. EMMA needs a 'feel' for how economic activity has been affected. Even very rough estimates of quantities can be useful.

8. Market-system analysis

Box 8.8 Comparing baseline and emergency trade volumes – example

The area worst affected by current flooding normally exports pulses (lentils) to the capital at this time of year. Flooding has severely damaged production. The export trade has stopped, and instead some pulses are now being imported into the district.

Baseline estimate

Consumption within district = 350 MT/month (national household survey)

Trade going out of district = 60 MT/month (reported by traders)

Therefore total production and trade = 410 MT/month

Emergency-affected estimate

Production within district = 200 MT/month (farm-damage reports)

Trade coming into district = 20 MT/month (interviews with traders)

Therefore total production and trade = 220 MT/month

Finding: total production and trade are down by approximately 50%.

With luck, enough data were collected (in Step 6) to make approximate estimates of emergency economic activity (production and trade volumes) at the local, provincial, and national scales.

Box 8.9 Analysis of baseline and emergency volumes – example

Volumes of production and trade (measured in MT per month)	National market	Provincial market	Local affected area
Baseline activity	5,000	1,200	200
Emergency-affected situation	5,000	1,100	50
Impact on production and trade	n/a	–10 %	–75 %

Interpretation: Production and trade in the disaster zone have been very severely affected by the emergency (down 75%). EMMA teams will need to understand the causes of this in detail, in order to assess prospects for a contribution by the local system to the emergency response. However, at the provincial market level, the change in activity has been fairly marginal (down only 10%), suggesting relatively minor impact on the system's capacity at that geographical level.

Supply problems and demand problems

Market systems work through the interaction between *demand* – people's ability to pay for goods or services that they need – and *supply* – other people's capacity to deliver those goods or services. It is therefore vital to understand how the emergency situation has affected this supply–demand dynamic.

In particular, it is vital to understand whether the changes in production and trade observed are essentially symptoms of demand problems, or supply problems, or a combination of both.

Demand-side and supply-side *problems* have very different impacts on target groups, depending on whether they are affected as consuming households, producers, or workers: hence there are different implications for humanitarian action.

Box 8.10 Demand-side and supply-side problems compared

Demand-side problems	*Supply-side problems*
In emergencies, effective demand (the level of spending by final consumers) is often affected. Most often, effective demand falls, because – whatever their urgent needs might be – final consumers have less money to spend.	Emergencies very often disrupt market systems' capacity to produce and deliver food, items, or services in response to demand. This may be due to problems at the production end of the chain; or it may be due to transaction blockages elsewhere in the market system.
Also, demand may fall because people receive sufficient relief distributions of that particular item, so they have less need to buy.	
	For example, a crisis may be linked to destruction of crops, or loss of warehouse stocks, or insecurity, or disruption of transport.
Occasionally demand may briefly increase: e.g. through a surge in purchases of food or shelter materials after a hurricane.	
	Occasionally, emergencies can also cause a problematic surge in supply (e.g. livestock sales during a drought).

8. Market-system analysis

How to do it qualitatively

The basic character of an emergency-affected market system's problems is usually assessed relatively easily from qualitative information collected in interviews with target groups and market actors.

The characterization of problems as supply- or demand-related depends on whether the market system is a supply system or an income system:

In supply market systems, demand depends on the ability and desire of the target population to purchase what they need. This assessment will come from the gap analysis (Step 7). Supplying food, items, or services to meet this demand is the role of the rest of the market system. Typical problems are presented in Box 8.11.

Box 8.11 Indicators of problems in 'supply' systems	
Demand-side problems (i.e. affecting target population)	*Supply-side problems* (i.e. affecting suppliers)
• Target households have less cash (or credit) than normal to spend. • Target households have restricted access to market actors or locations where critical food or items are available.	• Availability of the critical food, item, or service is significantly reduced. • Key market actors are badly affected. • Disruptions have occurred to transport links or other key infrastructure along the supply chain.

In income market systems, demand depends on the volume of purchases made by buyers and final consumers, or the amount of labour sought by employers, both of which generate income for the target population. Supply depends on the capacity of the target population to produce goods or labour for sale. Typical problems are listed in Box 8.12.

Box 8.12 Indicators of problems in 'income' systems	
Demand-side problems (i.e. affecting buyers)	*Supply-side problems* (i.e. affecting target population)
• Final consumers or other buyers are spending less on the critical product. • Employers are seeking less labour in the market system. • Key market-actors in the income value chain are badly affected. • Transport, storage, or key infrastructure along the value chain has been badly affected.	• Target households' production (e.g. cash crops) is significantly reduced, or they have less capacity to work (e.g. due to ill health, trauma). • Target households have more restricted access to output markets (e.g. transport constraints), or less access to employment markets (e.g. displacement). • There is an excessive supply of produce (e.g. livestock) or labour for sale.

How to do it quantitatively

EMMA can also use data about price changes and volumes of production and trade volume as indicators of what is happening to supply and demand in a market system *as compared with the baseline*. This can reinforce the assessment made qualitatively above.

It is also useful to look at the direction and pace of prices changes. Whether prices are generally rising, falling, or remaining stable can be as important as a direct comparison with the baseline situation. The table in Box 8.13 provides a key to this method.

The implications of supply-and-demand problems for emergency response are discussed further in Step 9. For a more economically rigorous but time-consuming approach to this topic, see the MIFIRA decision-tree tool (Barrett *et al.*, 2009), developed for CARE.

Box 8.13 Using data to diagnose supply-and-demand problems			
	Prices rising or much higher than baseline	*Prices stable and similar to baseline*	*Prices falling or much lower than baseline*
Volumes higher than baseline	*Demand is very strong. Supply response is good.* Indicates market system is performing well. However, high prices suggest that suppliers are still unable to satisfy surge in demand, or there are bottlenecks that raise costs for traders.	*Demand is strong. Supply response is good.* Indicates market system is performing well, compared with baseline: meeting increased needs, without creating price distortions.	*Demand is normal. Supply is excessive.* Indicates system is being saturated by over-supply. This is most likely where desperation forces people to sell labour, livestock, or assets on poor terms.
Volumes similar to baseline	*Demand is strong. Supply response is constrained.* Indicates trade levels are normal, but insufficient to satisfy increased demand. Alternatively, bottlenecks are raising costs for traders.	*Demand is normal. Supply is normal.* Indicates that market system is little affected, compared with the baseline situation.	*Demand is relatively weak. Supply is normal.* Indicates (income) market system is being saturated due to weak demand.
Volumes lower than baseline	*Demand normal (or strong). Supply response weak.* Indicates supply problems are very severe. Despite high prices, supply is insufficient to satisfy either normal or increased demand.	*Demand is weak. Supply response is uncertain.* Indicates that demand is constrained: buyers probably lack spending capacity.	*Demand very weak. Supply response is uncertain.* Indicates that demand is highly constrained: buyers lack spending capacity.

8. Market-system analysis

Bottlenecks in supply chains or value chains

If EMMA has reliable prices at different points along the supply chain or value chain, you can also use these to identify where bottlenecks are having an impact, by comparing changes in each actor's margin. A 'margin' is the difference between buying price and selling-on price.

In Box 8.14, the baseline margin of village traders = 5; the millers' margin = 20, and wholesalers' = 25.

Price margins normally reflect costs and risks borne by each different market actor (e.g. labour, transport, fuel, storage, credit). A dramatic change in the margin in the emergency situation can be a good indicator of a problem, constraint, or bottleneck in the supply chain or value chain at that point.

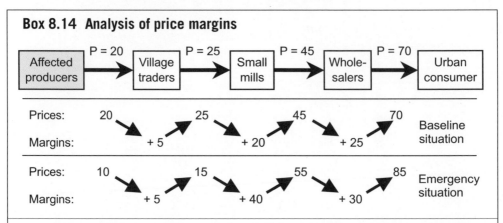

Box 8.14 Analysis of price margins

Interpretation: The emergency impact is that prices for producers are down, from 20 to 10; while consumer prices are up, from 70 to 85. How can this be explained? Analysis of margins for each intermediary shows that a bottleneck seems to occur with the millers: their margin has increased from 20 to 40. Other information may reveal the reason for this steep increase: for example, it may reflect the high cost of repairing milling machines, or the cost of running a generator because mains electricity has failed.

It is interesting to note that a 'demand constraint' (the millers' problems in Box 8.14) causes reduced income for producers. At the same time, the same problem creates a 'supply constraint' for the urban consumers, who face higher prices as a result. Either or both groups might be target groups for humanitarian assistance.

Reduced market integration

A market system that was well integrated in the baseline situation is more likely to be able to expand trade to meet emergency needs. However, market integration is often disrupted in an emergency. Identifying the causes and rectifying them can be an option to consider for emergency response.

EMMA teams will almost certainly not possess current price-series data to assess integration in the emergency situation (unless price monitoring began immediately). However, interviews with wholesalers, traders, and retailers will usually identify likely factors such as the following:

- damage to transport infrastructure (roads, bridges, waterways) affecting trade;
- elimination of key market actors who provided trade links with other markets;
- lack of finance for trading activities (break-down of credit arrangements);
- constraints on trade created by insecurity and conflict.

Protracted conflict often causes market fragmentation and the emergence of parallel or shadow markets in a war-distorted economy.

Changes in competition and market power

Abuse of market power presents a major risk for some emergency-response options.

- In supply systems, collusion between traders could cause prices to rise (or stay high), even though supplies are available and the market system is in other respects performing well.
- In income systems, lack of choice among buyers for producers and employers for workers can keep prices and wages down, even though healthy end-markets and work opportunities exist.

EMMA needs to assess how the emergency has affected competition and other positive and negative aspects of conduct. A crisis may knock out some businesses in the system and so reduce competitiveness among those remaining. It may destroy traders' capacity to offer usual services, loans, or credit. Alternatively, if social cohesion is strong, an emergency may temporarily improve people's conduct, as a sense of solidarity with the affected population takes hold.

Factors to look out for may include the following.

- *Reduced competition*: affected households have a restricted choice of suppliers (retailers, traders). Look at information on reduced numbers of market actors in the market map.
- *Increased monopolistic behaviour*: signs of collusion by groups of traders (cartels) to influence prices in their favour.
- *Damage to embedded services*, such as credit or other services that wholesalers, traders, or retailers offer to their customers, or employers to their employees.
- *Increased business risks* from loss of guaranteed sales or loan advances.
- *Greater exclusion*: worse restrictions on where and when certain market actors can trade.
- *Greater market distortion*: actions by governments (or humanitarian agencies) which temporarily disadvantage vulnerable producers or depress economic activity.

8. Market-system analysis

8.5 Prospects for contributing to the emergency response

By this stage, EMMA teams should be fairly confident they understand
- *how it was before:* the market system's baseline capacity and performance;
- *what has happened:* the impact of the emergency on the market system; and in particular an analysis of supply-and-demand problems in the emergency-affected situation.

The next step in market-system analysis is to use the knowledge and insights discussed above to predict how well the system is likely to perform in future: its potential to contribute to the emergency response at local, provincial, or national levels.

This is also where EMMA teams answer many of the key analytical questions first posed in section 2.4. There is no blue-print for making this kind of prediction or prognosis: this is a matter of judgement.

In addition, in supply systems EMMA will need to draw on information about
- *availability:* what stocks of the critical food or item exist, where they are located, and how quickly they can be mobilized by the market system.

Initial qualitative assessment

Without analysis of data, EMMA teams may be able to use market maps (and the information from interviews which they represent) to sketch conclusions about a critical market system's prospects for contributing to the emergency response. The essential character of emergency-affected market systems (i.e. supply-constrained or demand-constrained) will be an important aspect of this initial assessment.
- Example 1: A supply system serving a target population has suffered severe disruption, with damage to businesses or trade links that cannot be quickly repaired; and there are no obvious alternative market linkages. The system is characterized as supply-constrained: it is not likely that it will be able to fill the emergency gap. Therefore, in-kind distributions are needed.
- Example 2: A supply chain is relatively unscathed – any damage could be easily repaired – and market actors have stocks available. The emergency gap has emerged because the target population have lost their savings or normal sources of income. The local market system is characterized as demand-constrained: it could respond to the emergency gap if the target population, or humanitarian agency, had cash to spend. Therefore cash-based intervention or local procurement looks promising.

Comparison of gap analysis with production and trade volumes

Comparison of economic activity levels (both previously and in the emergency situation) with the gap analysis can be very revealing. In the example in Box 8.15, assume that the reduction in local trade is mainly due to households' lack of purchasing power (e.g. loss of income). Would the market system be capable of responding to demand if the target population had cash to buy what they need?

Box 8.15 Comparing 'gaps' with baseline volumes

Volumes of production and trade	Local affected area	Provincial market	National market
Emergency-affected situation (A)	50	1,100	5,000
Emergency gap identified (B)	350	350	350
Required response, A + B = (C)	400	1,450	5,350
Baseline activity (D)	200	1,200	5,000
Required increase over baseline = (C / D - 1) x 100 %	+ 100 %	+ 25 %	+ 8 %

Analysis of data in Box 8.15
The emergency response required to meet the gap (400 MT per month) is double the estimate of baseline production and trade in the affected area. The same gap is less challenging when put in the context of provincial markets (a 25% increase) and national markets (+ 8%).

Various implications can be drawn from this simple analysis in Box 8.15, including the following.

- It could be a significant challenge for local market actors to fill the emergency gap: even starting from the baseline situation, they would need to double their economic activity.
- Therefore unless there is evidence of strong integration between local and provincial markets, cash help for the target population would probably cause shortages and price rises in the local area.
- The provincial market system looks likely to have the necessary capacity to respond. Therefore procurement at this level is a more feasible option to consider. Availability and lead-times need to be checked.
- The national-level market seems unaffected, and procurement at this level also looks feasible. This could be the best option if the provincial market is supply-constrained.

Availability (stocks and lead-times)

Comparison of past or present trade volumes can lead EMMA teams to decide that market systems are NOT capable of responding to the emergency gap – thereby eliminating some response options. But in order to confirm that they *are* capable, EMMA also needs information about current availability (stocks) of the critical food or item. These essential data include the following factors:

- the stocks held by different types of market actor, including producers, along a supply chain;
- the lead-times (between order and delivery) expected at each link in the supply chain.

8. Market-system analysis

This information will come from the interviews with market actors (traders, retailers, etc.).

When investigating lead-time', treat people's responses with caution. Traders may exaggerate how quickly they can obtain supplies, in order to impress you, or they may be unaware of bottlenecks elsewhere. Always cross-check (triangulate) information with other market actors in the chain.

Information about availability can be usefully summarized and analysed in a table like Box 8.16. The information and data can be used to assess the availability at each of the economic scales of the market system – starting with the local affected area.

Box 8.16 Analysis of availability – example				
Required from Box 8.15	*National market* 5,500 MT/month + 8%	*Provincial market* 1,500 MT/month + 25%		*Local affected area* 400 MT/month + 100%
Actors	Farmers in other regions	Wholesalers and traders	Grain millers	Village retailers / Target households
Stock	Crops in fields	In ware-houses	Storage at mill	In shop stocks / Household stores
Quantity	> 30,000 tonnes	2,500 tonnes	600 tonnes	200 tonnes / 150 tonnes
Lead-times	6 weeks (harvest June)	1 week (transport)	2 weeks (milling bagging)	1 week (shop)

Local-market interpretation: Stocks in the local affected area (350 MT in homes and shops) could be expected to last only about one month in a cash programme or local procurement operation. This gives little time for retailers to receive extra stocks from millers, and in turn from wholesalers in the provincial market (the minimum lead-time is about three weeks). Therefore it would be essential to inform traders and millers about the local procurement or cash programme in advance. Since availability at the most local level is inadequate, the analysis must be taken to the provincial / regional level.

Provincial-market interpretation: The provincial stocks (approx 3,100 MT) are sufficient to meet the total required market response, including the gap for the target population in the affected area, for about two months. However, the total lead-time until the next national crop harvest is about nine weeks (refer to seasonal calendar). The provincial market may therefore need to bring in stocks from other areas before the normal harvest trade begins. If this still casts doubt on the system's capability, EMMA needs to look at the national situation.

National-market interpretation: The national production and trade system ought to manage an estimated 8% increase in demand relatively easily. However, the emergency response depends on the provincial traders being well integrated with the national market – so that they can procure supplies from other regions if necessary.

Analysis of national balance sheets

In major emergencies, the gaps may be so large that the national availability of stocks is a concern. National availability, rather than the market systems' capability to move critical stocks of food or items between unaffected and affected areas within the country, becomes the key issue.

For most staple food crops, national food balance sheets can be found through the FAOSTAT website http://faostat.fao.org. These provide national availability data against which emergency gaps can be assessed.

Conclusions: prospects for contributing to emergency response

Finally, the EMMA team must reach a conclusion about the capability of the market system to contribute to the emergency response. As noted earlier, this is essentially a question about where the most appropriate point of contact between humanitarian intervention and market system lies: at local, provincial, national, or international level.

This decision will be based on weighing up all the evidence and interpretations reached in Step 8 about the following factors:
* the characterization of the market systems' problems – whether supply-based or demand-based;
* past performance (baseline) and current activity;
* availability of stocks;
* degree of market integration at different levels;
* likely conduct of market actors (risks of abuse of market power).

In addition, the EMMA team should be able to answer many of the key analytical questions initially posed in section 2.4.

8.6 Market-support options

One of the distinctive features of the EMMA toolkit is that, beside enabling early decisions about direct response options (e.g. cash vs in-kind distributions), it explores opportunities for alternative forms of *indirect market support* that could rehabilitate or assist recovery of critical market systems. See Box 8.17.

Box 8.17 Direct and indirect responses defined	
Direct responses	*Indirect responses (market-system support)*
Actions that make direct contact with emergency-affected households	Actions with others – e.g. traders, officials – to indirectly benefit affected households
• Distributions of food or goods • Cash or voucher distributions • Cash-for-Work, Food-for-Work programmes • Provision of shelter, water, or sanitation • Nutrition programmes	• Rehabilitation of key infrastructure, transport links, bridges • Grants (or loans) for local businesses to restore stocks, rehabilitate premises or vehicles • Provision of technical expertise to local businesses, employers, or service providers.

The final component of Step 8 is to compile a long-list of all the indirect-response options which have emerged during the EMMA process. Consider all the ideas, proposals, and requests for assistance reported by target households, by market actors interviewed in the fieldwork, and by key informants; as well as the insights of the EMMA team.

These ideas are material for Step 9. Every proposal / option for market support should

• have obvious relevance to the target population (see Box 8.7);

• be identifiable with a clearly identified constraint or bottleneck in the market system;

• be consistent with the conclusions reached above (section 8.5) about market-system capability at different levels.

There is no benefit in trying to fix constraints at (for example) the village level, if the system still has more important, binding constraints at (for example) the regional level which prevent it contributing to response.

The results of this review of ideas can be collated in a table like Box 8.18.

Box 8.18 List of market-support options – examples

Market-system constraint	Proposed market-support options
Target groups have limited access to livestock market places, due to insecurity.	• Arrange safe conduct to market places. • Provide temporary livestock shelters and fodder.
Roads between the main rural trading hub and the provincial city are blocked by landslides.	• Organize public-works projects to clear debris, using cash-for-work mechanism.
Pre-season credit for agricultural inputs from wholesalers and retailers is not available.	• Distribute seed and fertilizers to farmers. • Guarantee business loans for traders. • Set up a voucher system to give wide access.
Traders cannot rent trucks for transporting goods, due to competition from aid agencies.	• Negotiate better logistics arrangements among agencies. • Bring in more vehicles to the area.
Vendors have been banned from the displaced people's camps by officials, or must pay high bribes.	• Advocate for changes to camp rules and official practices.

Checklist for Step 8

o   Baseline analysis: assessment of the market system's prior capacity and performance

o   Impact analysis: exploration of the impact of the emergency

o   Assessment of the market system's demand-and-supply problems

o   Future forecast: interpretations leading to estimates of market system's capacity to contribute to emergency response

o   Initial identification of market-support options

8. Market-system analysis

STEP 9

Response analysis

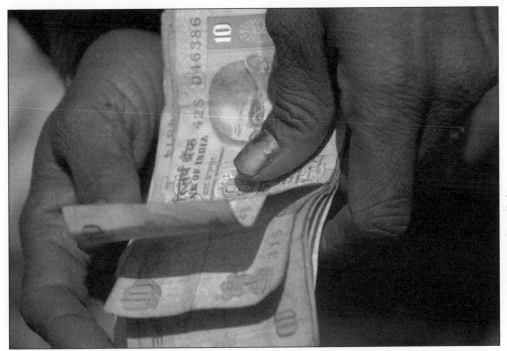

Money exchanging hands at the fish market in Uttar Pradesh, India.

The purpose of Step 9 is to produce response-option recommendations for agencies seeking to meet the emergency needs of a range of target groups. The essential task in response analysis is to move in a logical way from a position of understanding the emergency situation (Steps 6, 7, and 8) to making a set of reasoned recommendations for action. The logic of EMMA's response analysis is to examine the gap-analysis findings in the context of the market system's expected capacity to play its role in meeting the gaps. Where this capacity has been affected by the crisis, options for restoring it are explored.

> **Before starting Step 9, you will have...**
> o   consulted market actors and key informants about possible market-support actions;
> o   analysed supply-and-demand problems in the market system;
> o   assessed the market system's expected capacity to contribute to the emergency response;
> o   listed any plausible emergency market-support options to reinforce this capacity.

9.1 Overview of Step 9

Objectives

- Determine what response logic is most appropriate in each critical market system.
- Decide what type of direct assistance or other kinds of indirect action, including further investigation, to recommend.
- Estimate how much assistance is required.
- Describe when, and for how long, assistance or other indirect support should be provided, and how its impact could be monitored.

Activities

Section 9.2: Core logic of response
- Decide whether responses can or cannot rely on the market system performing well.

Sections 9.3–9.6: Response options
- Consider various options for response arising from the response logic.
- Appraise the options for market-system support identified during fieldwork.

Sections 9.7 and 9.8: Response frameworks
- Examine the feasibility and risks of the most attractive or plausible response options.
- Describe anticipated outcomes (and indicators for monitoring these).
- Summarize findings, interpretations, and conclusions.

Box 9.1 Response-analysis principles

Response analysis should follow the principle of providing assistance to target populations in direct proportion to need. This means not just filling a gap, but doing so in a way that builds on and supports people's livelihood strategies, including the local economic environment on which they rely in the longer term. Therefore response analysis should identify a pragmatic set of final options for action which are appropriate to the following:
- the implementing agency's goals and internal capacities (see Step 1)

- the needs and livelihoods of the affected population (see Step 7)

- the humanitarian operating environment, including the market system's capabilities (Step 8).

Key outputs

The results of this step will be expressed in two related response frameworks, described in the introductory chapter.

Response-options framework (Box 0.23)

The first framework summarizes information about the full range of plausible response options emerging as information from the EMMA fieldwork, and insights from your analysis. These response options may include both

- *direct* in-kind or cash-based assistance to target groups, and
- *in-direct* market-support options for restoring or bolstering the market system's capabilities (refer to Box 8.17 for definitions of direct and in-direct response).

Response-recommendations framework (Box 0.24)

The second framework presents to decision makers a small number of the most feasible response recommendations. These may include a combination of activities identified in the options framework.

9.2 The core logic of EMMA's response analysis

Up to now in EMMA (e.g. Boxes 0.2 and 2.2), humanitarian objectives in emergencies were roughly organized into three categories:

- *Meeting basic survival needs* (also known as 'livelihood provisioning') i.e. enabling households' access to safe water, food, shelter, clothing, sanitation.
- *Protecting livelihood assets and food-security capabilities* i.e. ensuring households' ability to produce own food, access water and fuel, and conduct other essential livelihood activities, including being available for work.
- *Promoting economic livelihoods, supporting recovery, and restoring income* i.e. restoring households' capacity to derive income from the sale of produce, or earn wages from employment.

These distinctions were useful, especially for informing the thinking that you used in order to select critical market systems. As we have seen, affected target groups may use these critical market systems either as a source of food, essential items, assets, and services (*supply*), or as a source of remuneration (*income*) for their own labour and produce.

However, when it comes to response analysis, it is useful to consider a different kind of categorization. EMMA's response options (the *actions*, not the objectives) depend on the relationship between humanitarian intervention and the respective market system. These actions fall into four categories:

(A) responses that rely on local market systems performing well (section 9.3);
(B) responses that aim to strengthen or support local market systems, so that actions in category (A) are more effective, less risky, or simply unnecessary (section 9.4);

9.
Response
analysis

(C) responses that do not rely on local market systems performing well (section 9.5);

(D) actions leading to further investigation, analysis, and monitoring (section 9.6).

Box 9.2 Different response options – example

Firewood needs in an IDP camp

Households in a rapidly expanding IDP camp are suffering acute shortage of fuel for cooking. Humanitarian concerns include local environmental degradation, risks to children and women scavenging firewood, and the potential for conflict with the host community. Depending on its assessment of the local firewood market system's capacity to respond to the IDP's needs, an EMMA study might identify the following response options.

If the market system is expected to perform well (A)

• Include a cash allocation for firewood in regular transfers to women householders.
• Create a voucher system to enable IDPs to purchase firewood at subsidized prices.

If the market system needs to be strengthened or supported (B)

• Negotiate official access to forestry reserves for authorized firewood traders.
• Guarantee loans and vehicle leases to enable more traders to enter the market quickly.

If the market system is not going to be capable of performing well (C)

• Distribute fuel-efficient stoves, to reduce households' firewood needs.
• Procure and distribute firewood rations to households in the camp.

If further investigation and analysis are needed (D)

• Continue to monitor prices of firewood inside the camp and in neighbouring towns, to confirm that EMMA's assessment of market-system capacity is accurate.
• Investigate the local market system for alternative cooking fuels (e.g. gas canisters).

EMMA's perspective is that all humanitarian objectives may require interaction with critical market systems at some level: local, regional, national, or international. For example:

• large-scale relief distributions rely on international market systems, or aid-donating countries;

- local in-country procurement depends on national or provincial level markets;
- cash-based interventions rely on market systems working right down to the local level in the emergency-affected area where the target population is located.

The question for EMMA users therefore is *'Which level is the most appropriate point of intervention for humanitarian action?'* This decision also depends on the scope for actions to support the local or national market system to work better: i.e. to be more efficient, integrated, equitable, and inclusive. Recall that the primary reasons for using EMMA (section 0.2) include:

- to make early decisions about the relative wisdom of in-kind distributions versus cash-based assistance for direct assistance to target households, and
- to assess opportunities for complementary 'indirect' actions, especially actions that strengthen the market system's capacity to respond to gaps.

The EMMA user's task is essentially therefore about deciding the extent to which the critical market system can be relied upon to play its role (as supply or buyer) in meeting a humanitarian objective. After Step 7, you should have a reasonable estimate of the gaps facing the target population. You should have a good-enough idea of the size of the shortfall between people's urgent needs and what this market system is currently delivering to them: between what people need to protect life and livelihoods, and what is available and accessible. You should also have a sense of what the shortfall is now, and what it is likely to be in the near future. By this stage, also, the EMMA team will probably have heard (from interviewees) or identified for themselves a range of ideas and proposals for emergency responses to this gap (see Box 8.18).

Response-decision tree

The decision process for selecting from these four options has a *core logic*, which can be summarized in three relatively simple analytical questions.

1. *Baseline situation*: How well did this market system work before the emergency?
   i.e. to what extent did it meet normal needs? How inclusive and accessible was it? How efficient, reliable, and fair was it? (market power)
2. *Impact of the crisis*: How has this market system been affected by the crisis, and how have market actors or others responded to the emergency?
   i.e. what is the situation now – e.g. structure, performance, prices, access, availability, conduct? What are the coping strategies? What are the existing humanitarian responses?
3. *Market-system forecast*: How well is this market system likely to react or respond to various proposed humanitarian actions, or other future impacts of the crisis?
   i.e. what will happen to demand, prices, access, availability in the market system if the affected population is given cash-type assistance? Or is assisted

with in-kind relief distributions? Or as a result of other expected future impacts of the crisis?

The diagrams in Boxes 9.3 and 9.5 illustrate this core logic, by showing how these three questions relate to the category of response decision. The form that these questions take differs between 'supply' and 'income' market systems.

Logic in supply market systems

In a supply system, the baseline question *'Did it work well before?'* asks whether the critical goods were generally available in sufficient quantities to satisfy the target population's actual spending ability (their effective demand). Note: a well-functioning supply market system does not imply that everyone including the poorest were able to afford what they needed. It only means that, where effective demand existed, the market system was able to respond to that demand reasonably well. This was indicated by the availability of goods, by the absence of monopoly behaviour (abuse of market power), and by prices being similar to those in comparable markets. All of these subjects were covered in Step 8.

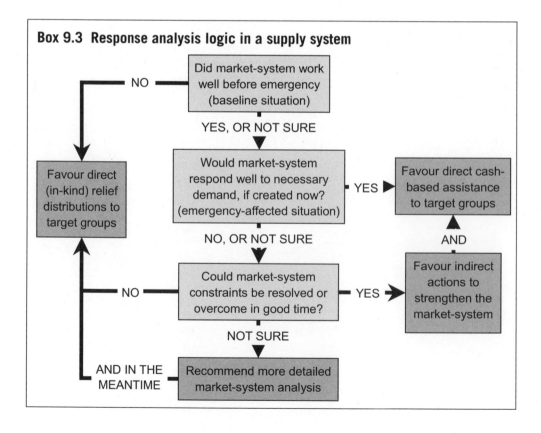

Box 9.3 Response analysis logic in a supply system

The impact question *'Would it respond well now?'* asks whether the market system would probably be able to satisfy the higher demand that would be created if the target population had more money to spend at a local level (i.e. after a cash-based intervention). In particular, whether it could do so without this increased local demand leading to an unreasonable rise in prices (e.g. by more than normal seasonal fluctuations, see Box 9.4).

Box 9.4 Reasonable prices?

A key issue for humanitarian agencies using cash or local procurement is to avoid doing harm by driving up prices. Markets can supply almost anything if the price offered is high enough. But by paying excessive prices (directly through procurement, or indirectly through cash-based interventions), humanitarian agencies risk merely diverting goods to the target population by depriving other groups who lack the same assistance.

However, it is also reasonable to expect supplier prices in an emergency situation to be higher than in the baseline. Traders may face greater costs and risks than normal – for example in transport and storage. EMMA's assessment of what is a 'reasonable price', based on information about costs and bottlenecks faced by traders, must take these factors into account.

The indicators of a market system's capacity to respond to emergency needs – and the necessary demand that this creates – were explored in Step 8. They include availability of stocks, absence of irresolvable bottlenecks; and fair levels of competition. *'Necessary demand'* refers to the total spending capacity (including that created by cash or voucher programmes) that the target population would need to have in order to fully address their supply 'gap' emergency needs. This subject was covered in Step 7.

Finally, the forecast question *'Could constraints be overcome in good time?'* asks whether bottlenecks or constraints could be overcome within the timeframe dictated by the humanitarian context: emergency needs and operational considerations. This subject was covered in Step 8.

Logic in income market systems

The decision tree is slightly different, but the logic is the same as for supply markets. Instead of food and items needed by the target population, the questions refer to the market demand for the sale of their own produce, crops, livestock, or labour.

9.
Response
analysis

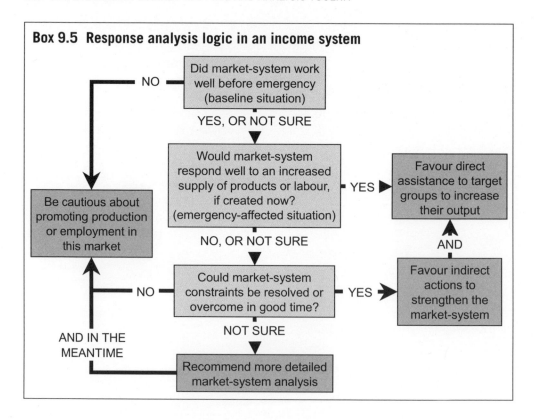

Box 9.5 Response analysis logic in an income system

In an income system, the baseline question *'Did it work well before?'* asks whether the target population was able before the crisis to find sufficient buyers at reasonable prices for their produce (or labour). Note: a well-functioning income market system does not imply full employment or good incomes for all. It only means that the market system was able to respond to availability of labour or produce with reasonable efficiency. This was indicated by the volume of purchases or employment, by the absence of monopoly behaviour (abuse of market power), and by prices being similar to those in comparable markets.

The impact question *'Would it respond well now?'* asks whether the market system's buyers would probably purchase restored or higher outputs. Alternatively, it asks whether employers would absorb increased labour, if available from the target population. For example, after support for productive activities, or job-seeking or skills-development activities.

In particular, it asks whether the market system could absorb this increased supply, without causing an excessive fall in prices or wages (e.g. by more than normal seasonal fluctuations). As discussed in Step 8, the indications of this capacity include availability of buyers (demand), absence of irresolvable bottlenecks; and fair levels of competition.

Finally, the forecast question *'Could constraints be overcome in good time?'* asks whether key bottlenecks or constraints that limit the market system's response could be overcome within the timeframe dictated by the humanitarian context: emergency needs and operational considerations.

9.3 Options when market systems are expected to work well

The first category of EMMA results consists of those where the critical market system is judged to be already capable of responding well to the target population's needs and gaps. In these cases, humanitarian agencies have the greatest range of options for action. Response choices can be based largely on non-market considerations, for example households' preferences for the form that assistance takes.

Humanitarian agencies may still choose to use non-market-based responses (e.g. in-kind distributions), for all kinds of operational reasons. However, in choosing to by-pass a market system, they bear a responsibility for any harm that might arise (for example, from undermining producers' prices, or increasing dependency), and missed opportunities to bolster the longer-term viability of producers, traders, businesses, or other market actors in that system (see Box 0.4).

Options in supply market systems

• Actors in this system are expected to be capable of supplying the gaps facing the target population, with or without supporting actions (see Boxes 8.11 and 8.12).

• Any system constraints that are currently inhibiting supply are capable of being resolved in good time (see section 9.4).

This type of finding encourages response options that directly tackle the target population's lack of spending capacity. These response options include cash transfers; voucher schemes; and cash-for-work programmes.

Box 9.6 Responses when supply systems are forecast to work well		
Options	*Description*	*Comparative advantages and disadvantages*
Cash transfers	Grants direct to target households	Needs are simple to assess. Assistance is easy to track and disburse, and monitoring receipt of funds is easy. Flexible and empowering for beneficiaries. Higher risk of misuse, especially in situations of conflict or power imbalances. Risk of inflation if supply constraints were overlooked or not resolved. Difficult to monitor use.
Voucher schemes	Tokens direct to households, valid for specific goods, shops, or traders	Compared with cash: easier to ensure agency's own humanitarian priorities. May mitigate insecurity concerns and risk of inflationary price rises in other markets. Need to assess business partners; set up and manage a repayment system with shops/traders.
Cash-for-work (1)	Paid short-term work available to all population	Easy to set up quickly and create a brief, rapid infusion of money into the local economy. Often more culturally and politically acceptable (dignified) than cash grants. Works undertaken may be useful for recovery. Work may be inaccessible for most vulnerable households, or be an unnecessary diversion from more useful activities.
Cash-for-work (2)	Paid longer-term work for the most vulnerable households only	Social programmes designed to reach vulnerable households and support them over a longer timeframe into recovery phase. More difficult to design well. Must be sensitive to social norms and perceptions of bias. Risk of creating long-term dependency or stigma.
Micro-credit	Small loans for replacement of assets though local savings groups	With care, reinforces local institutions and social capital – contributes to longer-term recovery. May exclude the more vulnerable, socially marginalized. Risk of overloading saving groups' management capabilities.

Cash and voucher schemes

A great deal of guidance is now available on the operational design and implementation of cash and voucher programmes. Some of these are available on the accompanying EMMA reference manual. For further reading, see:

- Oxfam's *Cash-transfer Programming in Emergencies* (Creti and Jaspars, 2006)
- ICRC's *Guidelines for Cash-Transfer Programming* (ICRC, 2007)
- ACF's *Implementing Cash-based Interventions* (ACF International Network, 2007)

Cash-for-work programmes

When considering cash-for-work as a response option, it is important to be clear what objective you have in mind. Mercy Corps, for example, identify three different types of CfW response, with different goals and operational implications (refer to Box 9.7).

9.
Response
analysis

Box 9.7 Three different objectives of cash-for-work

1. CfW to kick-start the local economy

Used to inject money (liquidity) rapidly into the local economy, for example after a sudden shock. The primary objective here is to kick-start economic activity: by re-stimulating demand and thus helping to revive trading, production, and employment. These responses are fast, short-term (20–30 days), and universal. Work opportunities are made available to all households, at around 80 per cent of a normal local wage. The nature of the work is less important than its accessibility to all target groups. From EMMA's perspective, the key concern is to ensure that constrained demand (see Box 8.14) has been correctly identified as the only major problem in the critical market systems: for example, because the target population have lost their savings or normal sources of income. If there are other supply constraints, then a rapid infusion of cash into the local economy carries the risk of causing price rises.

2. CfW to support the most vulnerable households in medium term

Used as a form of medium-term income support for the most vulnerable. The primary objective here is the welfare of target groups. This involves relatively small payments to help households to meet basic needs over the course of several months, a year, or longer. This kind of cash-based response is targeted at extra-vulnerable households, so the nature of the work must be appropriate and accessible. It is often supplemented by other relief activities, related, for example, to nutrition or education. From EMMA's perspective, the risk of market distortions (price rises) is lower than other types of CfW, since the number of beneficiaries and the sums involved are usually relatively small, or spread out over time. This, in turn, places less demand on the local capacity of critical market systems to respond.

3. CfW to conduct essential tasks / public works

Used to recruit labour to achieve specific emergency or recovery-related tasks: for example, clearing debris, repairing key roads and bridges, public shelters, water and sanitation infrastructure. Most often used for communal or public assets; but might also be appropriate for rehabilitation of private property (e.g. irrigation system, landing jetty), if this is critical to the performance of a market system on which a target group depends. This response usually requires technical supervision; is not on a very large scale; lasts only as long as necessary; and employs those most able to do the work.

From EMMA's perspective, a key concern is not to draw labour away from other important activities in the local economy. Therefore, responses should pay wages that are close to local market norms, should minimize the programme scale and duration, and should schedule programmes to fit the seasonal calendar.

Source: Dee Goluba, Mercy Corps

Micro-credit for asset replacement

Where financial institutions, including informal savings and revolving-loan groups, are still functioning, it may be feasible to channel cash assistance through them. Capital grants to organizations can enable them to offer increased loans, or temporary repayment holidays, to members.

Care must be taken to ensure that the groups or institutions have the technical and political capacity to manage the volume of assistance to be delivered. It is easy to overwhelm informal organizations and undermine carefully nurtured cultures of repayment responsibility.

For further reading, see the section on financial-services standards in *Minimum Standards for Economic Recovery after Crisis* (SEEP Network, 2009).

Options in income market systems

Actors in the system are expected to be willing and able to purchase extra produce or labour from the target population, either with or without support.

Any system constraints that are currently inhibiting demand from buyers or employers are capable of being resolved in good time (see section 9.4).

This conclusion gives a green light to response options that directly tackle the target population's limited or restricted productive capacity. These response options aim to increase output and promote employment and income-generating activities. They include facilitating replacement of productive assets, and provision of inputs and key services or skills (see Box 9.8).

In general, this type of situation leads agencies into the area of value-chain development work. For further reading, see Campbell (2008), Miehlbradt and Jones (2006), and the Microlinks site listed in Box 1.2.

Box 9.8 Producers' needs when income systems are forecast to work well	
Category	*Examples*
Replacement of productive assets	Farming implements, hand tools, fishing tackle, livestock
Provision of essential inputs	Seeds, fertilizers, animal fodder, nutritional supplements, productive materials
Provision of key services	Transport services, safe market places, agri-extension advice, veterinary services (e.g. vaccination of livestock)
Skills development	Training in specific vocational skills

9.
Response
analysis

Inter-linked income and supply market systems

Suppose that EMMA finds significant opportunities for target groups in income market systems. A key decision will then be how best to facilitate these target groups' access to the assets, inputs, or services needed to take advantage of these opportunities. For example, a healthy market demand for fresh fish raises the question: how best to assist fisherfolk to replace boats and nets? Similarly, strong buyer demand for milk may create in turn a demand for supply of animal fodder and nutritional supplements.

This illustrates the inter-linked relationship between critical income systems for producers and the supply systems that might provide them with vital inputs and services. Healthy demand and a well-functioning income system create an economic opportunity. This means that the related supply systems are then also critical.

In these circumstances, EMMA teams need to focus attention on these input-supply systems. You need to investigate whether or not they can be expected to work well also. If they can, then some of the same options for cash-based interventions (in Box 9.6) can be considered: particularly cash transfers, vouchers, or micro-credit.

9.4 Options when market systems need supporting or strengthening

The second category of EMMA results consists of those where the critical market system is judged to be potentially capable of responding well to the target population's needs and gaps, but its current capacity is limited by constraints that could be rectified in good time.

The market system may still be able to play an effective role in the emergency response (as in section 9.3), if these constraints are amenable to practical and quick solutions.

Evidence that a critical market system has good potential to respond:
- Production and trade volumes achieved in the baseline situation would be sufficient to meet emergency needs now, if restored.
- Market actors are convinced of their inherent capacity to supply / buy adequately.
- The bottlenecks or constraints that restrict production or trade are clearly apparent and amenable to action.

In these circumstances it makes little difference whether EMMA is investigating a supply market system or an income market system. The response options will arise from whatever very specific issues and problems the market actors are facing and have reported.

Box 9.9 Service provision or market facilitation

The approach described in this section describes situations in which agencies seek to support actors in market systems to recover from crisis or strengthen themselves. This is very different from conventional humanitarian responses which displace market actors by substituting for them – taking up the very roles or activities on which their businesses and livelihoods rely. A huge body of experience and guidance is now available on market-development approaches, including value-chain development. Recently the emerging lessons and principles of these approaches have begun to be applied to emergency situations.

See Minimum Standards for Economic Recovery after Crisis *(SEEP Network, 2009) and www.bdsknowledge.org for resources on market development generally.*

A key lesson from the market-development field is that intervening agencies need to shift their role from that of 'service provider' to that of temporary 'facilitator'. Facilitators seek to avoid creating unsustainable aid-dependency by minimizing their direct role in the market system, and the duration of their intervention. At the same time, the facilitator indirectly encourages and supports market actors to recover or take up the roles and activities that are needed for the market system to perform well for the target population.

In many emergency situations, humanitarian agencies cannot afford to stand back and merely facilitate. However, where market systems are (close to) working well, the scope for non-conventional action is greater: that is the ethos in this section of EMMA.

Infrastructure rehabilitation

The first category of market-system support is rehabilitation of key infrastructure. This might include not only public infrastructure (water and sanitation systems, roads, bridges, electricity supplies) but also trading infrastructure that plays a key role in market-system performance: for example, market places, storage facilities and premises, livestock-trading facilities. EMMA teams may identify infrastructure priorities, e.g. restoring electricity services or road access to a key grain mill, which are overlooked in conventional humanitarian priorities. In some circumstances EMMA might propose the rehabilitation of privately owned assets – for example land, ponds, irrigation ditches, jetties, ice-making facilities – if these are essential components of a critical market system on which many target households rely.

Humanitarian agencies that are considering activities in this area need to liaise with local government. Public-infrastructure rehabilitation should be co-ordinated through government plans, and agencies should avoid replacing governments' primary role in this aspect of market-system rehabilitation as far as possible.

9.
Response
analysis

Box 9.10 Market-system support – rehabilitation of infrastructure	
Response options	*Examples*
Rehabilitation of public infrastructure	Public works to restore roads, bridges, port facilities, irrigation pumps, water tanks, electricity supply. Opportunities for cash-for-work (type 3 in Box 9.7)
Rehabilitation of market infrastructure	Grants or works to restore market stalls, kiosks, storage facilities, water, temporary market places, livestock markets
Rehabilitation of private infrastructure	Desalination and debris removal on agricultural land, reconstruction of fish ponds, drainage ditches, irrigation channels; construction of jetties

Financial services

Financial services, especially credit – in its many different forms – are the life-blood of all market systems. Most market actors, from the smallest farmer to the largest trader, rely on advances or credit for buying inputs, investing in stocks, and paying for transport in advance of sales. Credit relationships are closely linked to (embedded with) the trading of goods along supply chains or value chains. In emergency situations, disruption to the key credit providers in the chain can easily cause a 'credit crunch'. Therefore it may be just as vital to restore these financial linkages as it is to restore the physical or logistical ones.

Box 9.11 Market-system support – financial services	
Direct business grants / loans	Grants, loans, or in-kind material assistance for reconstruction of premises, re-stocking, for purchasing inputs, for transport of goods
Guarantees for traders	Letters of credit or other financial guarantees to support traders to re-establish business or negotiate new lines of credit from their suppliers (e.g. for importers of critical food / essential items)
Support for producer groups	Grants or loans to producer associations (guilds, marketing co-operatives, unions) to facilitate increased economic activity
Support for micro-finance institutions	Capital grants (or loans) to bolster financial institutions during period of stress (non-payment of premiums). Temporary financing for credit unions

Many humanitarian agencies hesitate to consider providing loans or grants directly to market actors (for example, local retailers) who are relatively wealthy compared with the target population. However, this may logically be the most efficient way to restore a market system's performance. There may be imaginative solutions – such as supporting a local micro-finance institution with capital, or providing letters of credit – which avoid the worst of these dilemmas. Voucher schemes, for example, are also a useful mechanism that can be linked to support for particular vital traders in a supply chain. For further reading, see *Minimum Standards for Economic Recovery after Crisis* (SEEP Network, 2009).

Business services and transport

It may be justified in critical market systems to provide inputs and services on an emergency basis directly to market actors who are not in the target population. Transport bottlenecks are a common constraint, especially in conflict situations. Directly assisting key traders and transporters to restore the movement of critical goods (and sometimes of people too) may be an efficient humanitarian solution.

Other vital business services (non-financial) might include helping key market actors to overcome bureaucratic obstacles, such as having to obtain transit permits and business licences (e.g. registration to operate in a refugee camp).

Box 9.12 Market-system support – business services	
Support for transport services	Protective convoys in conflict zones. Vouchers for fuel. Help with leasing of vehicles to traders
Support to deal with bureaucracy	Practical administrative or lobbying support to help to overcome bureaucratic obstacles, obtain business licences, transit permits, etc.
Wholesale supply to traders	Legal or logistical help with importing goods (food, essential items, material) into an emergency area. Sale (monetization) of food aid into local markets where local supply is constrained

Agricultural inputs and extension services

Agricultural 'income' market systems (including livestock and fishery sectors) are often critical in emergency situations – as a source of employment for poorer and landless rural households, as a source of income for small farmers and fisherfolk, and for ensuring future food availability. A wide variety of inputs supply chains and extension services (both public and private) are often involved in enabling these systems to work well for producers in normal circumstances. Where emergencies disrupt these inputs and services, but the demand for the end products is still strong, EMMA teams may recommend temporary emergency responses in compensation.

9. Response analysis

Note: sometimes input supply chains are so vital to target populations directly (for example, seed suppliers for subsistence-level food producers) that they should probably be selected as critical market systems for investigation in their own right (Step 2). The need for repeated or long-term humanitarian interventions to support such services indicates the need for more detailed analysis of the problems. See Sperling (2008) for analysis of 'seed systems', for example.

Box 9.13 Market-system support – agricultural inputs and services	
Seed and input programmes	Emergency seed programmes; related provision of fertilizers and tools. Support for seed fairs, rehabilitation of seed and tree nurseries
Livestock services	Vaccinations, supplementary feeding, access to fodder, temporary protection and shelter
Livestock markets	De-stocking to manage demand, improvements to market place / trading centre facilities, re-stocking programmes
Agri-tools and machinery	Assistance with investments in tools, agro-machinery, irrigation equipment. Advice and support (e.g. grants) to providers of agro-machinery rental services

Comprehensive advice on livestock programming has recently been published in the Sphere-associated Livestock Emergency Guidelines and Standards (LEGS). A useful review of the LEGS work (Watson and Catley, 2008) is included in the EMMA reference manual materials

Information services and lobbying

Humanitarian agencies can do a great deal in terms of facilitating access to information, and using their influence. The market-mapping process should have revealed the main obstacles that market actors face in the institutional environment (especially rules and regulations). Lack of access to basic information is also a common constraint.

Where a major humanitarian response is likely to be implemented, advance information is a key factor that enables market actors to respond appropriately. If cash programmes are planned, traders need time to order and secure fresh supplies.

Box 9.14 Market-system support – information and lobbying	
Market information services	Informing market actors about what is happening and planned by humanitarian agencies. Making available the results of monitoring – especially prices in different market locations
Market linkages	Building links between market actors, e.g. through trading events, seed fairs, market exhibitions
Employment agencies	Linking target groups to opportunities for employment, skills development, or vocational training
Business services	Help with licensing and regulations (e.g. camp rules); guidance on tendering for contracts
Advocacy and influence	Lobbying government officials for improvements in food-movement policy, tariff reductions, speed of import clearances, emergency tax holidays, safe passage for traders

9.5 Options when market systems are not expected to respond well

The third category of EMMA results consists of those where the critical market system is judged to be incapable of responding well to the target population's needs and gaps. The bottlenecks and constraints that it faces cannot be rectified in good time.

Options in non-performing income market systems

Discourage investment and production

When EMMA finds that an income market system – i.e. a potential source of income or employment for target groups – is not expected to respond well to a fresh supply of goods or labour, it is necessary to spell this out very clearly –otherwise wishful thinking and the urge to 'do something' for people can dominate decision making. The unsold products of ill-considered production initiatives ('Maybe we will find buyers for these tomatoes / goat-hides / handicrafts / tailored clothes') are a familiar sight.

If demand is insufficient or uncertain, EMMA teams should actively discourage investment in income-generating activities or production for that market system.

Respond to problems of over-supply

A special case of market-system failure in income markets happens when emergencies cause a surge in supply (rather than a collapse of demand). This can happen easily in casual labour markets – when target groups, e.g. displaced people, are suddenly forced to seek new ways of earning a living. It is also characteristic of livestock

9. Response analysis

markets, especially during severe droughts or conflict, when supplies of fodder dry up and people are forced to sell their animals quickly.

A legitimate response in such cases – if agencies have sufficient resources – is to try to temporarily soak up some of the excess supply of goods, livestock, or labour, by means such as the following:

- de-stocking programmes for livestock (see the LEGS Manual);
- temporary alternative employment (e.g. cash-for-work type 1 in Box 9.7);
- employer subsidies / incentives to protect jobs on private land / businesses.

Options in non-performing supply market systems

When EMMA finds that market systems are not capable of responding well to the target population's needs, then humanitarian agencies have no choice but to respond directly. These are, perhaps, the conventional emergency relief responses:

- food aid;
- distribution of essential household items, clothing, shelter materials ;
- distribution of agricultural tools, inputs, seeds, fodder;
- replacement of livelihood assets;
- re-stocking of livestock.

However, the understanding of the critical market system provided by EMMA may still be valuable in the medium or longer term. So, for example, your EMMA report may be able to advise or describe the following:

- when, or under what conditions, a critical market system is likely to have recovered sufficiently for humanitarian assistance to be switched to cash-based interventions (e.g. when transport link X is re-opened; or after the next harvest in area Y; or when traders return to market places in region Z);
- when, or under what conditions, relief distributions could be phased out;
- what indicators of market-system performance to continue monitoring (e.g. market prices in specific locations);
- any risks of harm that relief distributions might cause to particular market actors, and hence to the system's future performance, so these can be mitigated (e.g. distributions of food aid can be expected to create disincentives for farmers to plant next season's staple grain crops in region B).

9.6 Options when results are uncertain or more information is needed

The final category of EMMA results relates to situations where insufficient information and data are available to make a confident assessment of the critical market system's capacity to respond well to the target population's needs and gaps. Usually, precaution means that EMMA teams have to assume the worst and treat the situation as a non-performing market system (section 9.7).

However, if further investigation, which might take various forms, is possible, this can be recommended alongside relief distributions.

Establishing price monitoring

Even short-term price monitoring can reveal useful information about what is happening in market systems, especially if you can compare current price levels and movements with some approximate pre-emergency baseline. Exceptionally, it may even be possible to 'pilot test' market-based responses in a limited area that is carefully monitored to see what effect this has on local prices and market performance.

It is advisable to set up simple price-monitoring systems, whatever emergency-response options are recommended. This is an activity where collaboration with other agencies is vital, to avoid duplication and ensure that comparable data are collected.

Further advice on price monitoring and the interpretation and use of price-series data is given in the EMMA reference manual on the CD-ROM.

Investigating other (related) market systems

EMMA investigation in one critical market system may reveal the need for assessment in another, usually a related or interlinked system. For example, a study of inland fishery systems might reveal the critical role of the fish-net supply chain. This does not necessarily indicate a failure of system selection (Step 2): sometimes only detailed fieldwork with market actors on the ground reveals the importance of a related supply chain or service market. Fortunately, the groundwork for this kind of supplementary EMMA investigation will usually have been done already, so reducing the time and cost involved.

Terms of reference for specialist market analysis

Sometimes an EMMA investigation with its urgent, short-term timeframe turns out to be clearly leading the way towards a more substantial and longer-term programme. This is the transition from emergency programming to longer-term economic and livelihood recovery.

These transitions may justify the need for more detailed and quantified market analysis by specialists who have experience of the market sector. For example, an investigation of the milk market system for emergency-affected small dairy farmers indicates that there are significant opportunities to expand local production and get into higher-value products (e.g. cheese making). This is a longer-term proposition, which requires analysis by dairy-sector specialists and livelihoods advisers, using value-chain development methods for example.

In such circumstances, it is appropriate for EMMA teams to use the EMMA results to describe Terms of Reference (ToR) for further in-depth specialist analysis. Guidance on writing these kinds of ToR is included in the EMMA reference materials.

9.
Response
analysis

9.7 Response-options framework

The response-options framework is simply a device for recording and summarizing the most plausible response options that emerged from the EMMA fieldwork (Step 5) and response analysis. The purpose of the framework is to provide decision makers with a quick overview of all the reasonable options that the EMMA team considered and which can be included in a short report or presentation. (See Step 10.)

Box 9.15 shows an extract from the full example illustrated in Box 0.23.

Box 9.15 Response-options framework			
Option	*Advantages*	*Disadvantages*	*Feasibility and timing*
Relief distribution of spare supplies from Forest Dept.	Immediate impact. Would utilize existing / useless stocks; for the short term, will slow deforestation; simple distribution programme.	Requires warehouses, distribution staff. Limits integration with markets in town and camp. Wood may be sold on, not used.	Low! Expect lack of co-operation. 2–3 weeks to begin
Distribution involving camp-based retailers and vouchers	Inject cash into camp economy. Thus lots of secondary beneficiaries; would create more local vendors	Very few camp retailers with any capacity; no storage or infrastructure inside camps. Open to fraud. Start-up slow – with procurement and beneficiary-identification process	Medium. 2 months to implement
Refilling of gas canisters; conditional on school attendance	Less firewood usage; time-saving. Incentives for sending children to school. Reduces protection issues. Clear exit strategy: reduce distributions	Gas is twice the price of firewood; risky to use inside tents; IDPs cannot afford refilling on their own. May increase dependency on aid; makes school attendance linked to reward, instead of intrinsic worth; not sustainable	High. Can be started soon
Cash distribution to all IDP women household heads	Inject money into the camp economy; positive effect on HH economies, but no effect on firewood market; gives women choices	Potential for inflation; corruption; no exit strategy; no way to ensure that cash is used for firewood; women might continue to send children to collect firewood instead of buying it	Low. Quick response

Feasibility of options

EMMA teams need to provide an assessment of the relative advantages and disadvantages of each response option included in the framework. These should include the following, for example:

- What is the likely impact of proposed intervention on the market system (including the risk of causing price distortions)?
- What added risks or vulnerability does the proposal create – for example, in changing the burden on women's time?
- To what extent will this proposal support (or undermine) existing long-term interventions?

In addition, some indication of the practical operational feasibility of each proposal is important.

In the case of cash-programming options, detailed advice on operational feasibility is now available from many sources (ACF International Network, 2007; ICRC, 2007). See also the questions in Box 4.2, taken from Oxfam's cash-programming guidelines.

9.8 Response-recommendations framework

Finally, from the range of options summarized above, you can present the EMMA team's recommendations for emergency response (see Box 9.16). These may, of course, involve a combination of activities, such as cash-based intervention (section 9.3), with a set of market-system support actions (section 9.4).

Box 9.16	Response-recommendations framework			
Response activities or combinations	*Key risks and assumptions*	*Timing issues*	*Likely effect on market system and target groups*	*Indicators*
Fuel-efficient stoves and cooking techniques • Stove distribution • Cooking techniques • Sensitization on fuel efficiency, de-forestation, child-protection issues	Access to camps. People are willing to learn and use stoves. We can find training staff	1–2 months to make an impact	Decrease household firewood expenses. Increase fuel efficiency at household level. Small – but important – positive effect on environment. Improved protection (fewer children collecting wood)	# of stoves distributed and used by IDPs. Comparison of wood-fuel consumption, old vs new

Recommendations may also include phased activities – where different responses start at different times. This is particularly relevant to programmes that cover or anticipate a transition from emergency relief to economic recovery. Some examples of this can be found in Mercy Corps' guidelines on planning and transitional economic-recovery programmes in quick-onset emergencies (Mercy Corps, 2007).

Issues of timing

Indicate when activities need to begin – bearing seasonal factors in mind. Describe whether actions are one-off or continuous. If continuous, for how long they will be needed?

Appraisal of key risks and assumptions

Recommendations need to be accompanied by an appraisal of any predicted major risks, and the assumptions being made. It is impossible to avoid all risks, but comparisons between alternative options are more realistic if risks are acknowledged clearly. Significant external factors over which agencies have no control, such as expected government actions, or the likelihood of poor weather, can be gauged (e.g. likely, unlikely) and factored into the decision-making process.

Assumptions are essential in EMMA – since decisions have to be based on limited and partial information. The important thing is to record them: for example, 'Traders will be able to double the supply (availability) of critical items within four weeks'.

Impact indicators

As early as possible, when response options are being recommended, it is important to identify how the benefits arising from response activities will be measured and monitored throughout the course of an intervention. The identification of these indicators is, increasingly, a requirement of donors. They enable programmes to set outcome goals which can be used later to evaluate how successful assistance has been. See the OFDA guidelines for useful information on suitable indicators for donor proposal (OFDA, 2008).

More importantly, the monitoring of impact indicators will enable agencies to assess whether the response actions are creating the desired benefits for the target population. Bear in mind that improvements and deteriorations can also be caused by other factors out of your control, such as climate, market dynamics, and changes in the political or governance environment. This is vital where cash-based interventions or indirect activities such as market-system support are being proposed.

A key indicator in cash-based programmes should be the local prices of critical food or non-food items. Large or prolonged changes to prices (up or down) may be an indication that the market system is not performing as well as anticipated, prompting agencies to change tack.

For further guidance on price monitoring, see the EMMA reference manual.

Checklist for Step 9

o   Response-analysis logic – predicting if the market system will perform well.

o   Response options arising from the response logic.

o   Appraisal of the options for market-system support identified during fieldwork.

o   Feasibility and risks of the most attractive or plausible response options.

o   Response options and recommendation frameworks.

STEP 10
Communicating results

Tap stand in Swat Valley, Pakistan.

The purpose of Step 10 is to document the EMMA findings and communicate them in a timely and effective way to decision makers and other target audiences. The emphasis is on brief, convincing, visually accessible formats for reports or presentations.

Before starting Step 10, you will have...
o completed the gap-analysis, market-analysis, and response-analysis strands;
o arrived at your conclusions in the form of a response-recommendations framework.

10.1 Overview of Step 10

Objectives

- Write up the findings and conclusions of EMMA's investigation in a format that is useful and accessible to decision makers.
- Make the findings and conclusions available rapidly to an appropriate audience of managers, donors, and collaborating agencies.

Key outputs

- Executive briefing: two-page document summarizing findings and recommendations
- Presentation: 15–20 minute verbal / slide presentation
- Comprehensive EMMA report

10.2 Presenting EMMA results effectively

The audience for EMMA

Communicating the results of EMMA means ensuring that they feed into the key decision-making processes of your organization and those of others. Think carefully about who will use the EMMA results. Your audience may include emergency-programme planners and managers, colleagues in Cluster co-ordination meetings, internal fundraisers, donors who allocate resources, monitoring and evaluation staff, advocacy staff, and policy makers.

Most of these audiences are working under intense time-pressures, especially in a sudden-onset emergency situation. They need succinct, accessible, non-technical communication formats, targeted at the analysis users, and recommendations that can readily be translated into action.

The main EMMA tools – household economic profiles, market-system maps, and seasonal calendars – are important visual tools in this communication effort, in addition to the part they play in the analytical process. To maximize their effectiveness, you need to think about the needs of your audiences.

Box 10.1 Using results to get action – four rules of thumb

1. Decision makers have busy schedules and limited time.

A one- or two-page brief, or a presentation, or direct participation in decision makers' processes, is the best way to convey the minimum set of information with the maximum effect to people who can take action. Comprehensive reports have an important function, but they are not the right tool for translating information into action. Given the time constraints of most decision makers, it is not reasonable to expect anyone with a busy schedule to read a long detailed report.

2. Decision makers in the humanitarian community need to co-ordinate with others and require some consensus concerning their actions.

It is essential to engage in the processes and meetings that decision makers attend. This engagement allows you to bring information to the table as soon as it is generated, and it encourages trust and co-operation. In this context, when information that requires action is available, one of the most effective ways to convey it is through a joint presentation to the key decision makers (donors, NGOs, government, etc.) involved in funding, designing, and carrying out the required response.

3. Decision makers, once convinced, have to make their case to others repeatedly, and they need the ammunition to do so.

Be prepared to put together a series of briefing papers or notes in response to a decision maker's request. Think in terms of a press-kit approach, where saying the most in the least amount of time is critical. Try to imagine the kinds of question to which a decision maker might need quick responses, and then provide as many of these answers up front as possible.

4. Decision makers need significant lead time to acquire resources and to make logistical arrangements for interventions/projects.

The time between the end of an investigation and the issuing of a briefing note or presentation should be kept to a minimum. It is important to ensure that your information is provided in a coherent, concise, and logical way as early into the needs-assessment planning period as possible, in order to ensure that decision makers have an opportunity to incorporate it into their overall request to donors. This may require doing interim analyses, and then narrowing down the scope as more information becomes available. This can also help to whet the appetite of decision makers, and to generate a demand for more closely focused analyses as the season progresses.

Source: The Practitioner's Guide to the Household Economy Approach, FEG Consulting and Save the Children (2008).

For further guidance on how to present executive briefs and more detailed assessment reports, see Chapter 5 ('Translating outcomes into actions') in the same source.

10.
Communicate
results

10.3 Structure of an EMMA report

When presenting the results of EMMA, it is essential to provide answers to the key analytical questions with which you began in Step 3. Reports and presentations in any format (whether comprehensive or brief) should clearly answer these questions.

Examples of actual and model EMMA reports are provided in the EMMA reference manual.

Section 1: Executive summary, or brief

This is the key summary of EMMA's findings and recommendations. It concentrates on the outputs from Steps 6–9. Market-system maps (of baseline and emergency-affected situations) provide the foundation for the findings, backed up by household profiles and seasonal calendars if necessary. Recommendations are presented in the form of the response-option frameworks.

Section 2: Emergency context

This section is not essential for communicating to audiences on the ground (such as Cluster-group members); but in a more comprehensive report, for example to donors, the following information is vital in order to put the findings in context. It represents the outputs of Step 1 essentially, and consists of the following elements:

- a brief description of the emergency / crisis – its cause and impact;
- an explanation of the agency's role and geographical area of responsibility;
- key findings from emergency needs assessments;
- key background information concerning, for example, the socio-economy, livelihoods, political context (if appropriate) of the target population;
- a quick overview of humanitarian responses to date.

Section 3: EMMA methodology

A brief description (half a page) of the methodology used and activities undertaken to produce the report (Step 5) is vital for establishing credibility. It should cover the following topics:

- composition and experience of the team, and any training provided;
- fieldwork locations and methodology (e.g. number and types of interview);
- how leadership and support were provided to the EMMA team.

Section 4: The target population

This section summarizes the available information about the target population, including what was known before EMMA fieldwork (Step 1 preparatory information) and afterwards (Step 7):

- overview of target population: numbers, locations, livelihood profile, and general situation (refer to sections 1.5 and 7.2);
- target groups within the population: how disaggregated on particular lines, and why (sections 1.6 and 7.2);
- seasonal calendar(s) to illustrate key features of livelihoods, if relevant (section 7.5);
- impacts of the emergency on different target groups in general (e.g. changes in household income and expenditure profiles, from section 7.6 results) – a summary with links to an annex that contains the details.

Section 5: Critical market systems

This section summarizes the decision process that was undertaken in order to select specific critical market systems (Step 2). It explains – *briefly* – how you got from a general understanding of emergency needs to a list of candidates for market-system analysis.
- What are the critical market systems for the affected population – before and now? (section 2.2)
- Which systems will the EMMA team look at, and why have they been selected? (rationale from section 2.3)

Section 6: Market-system maps

This is the main descriptive section of the report, based on findings from Step 6. Try to keep it succinct. Use the system maps as much as possible, with brief explanations of the key features. Include both types of map:
- the baseline market-system map (section 6.2)
- the emergency-affected market-system map(s) (section 6.3).

Where the maps are complex and you want to illustrate different issues, it may be better to have different maps. For example, one map could show the trade volumes (quantities) at different points in the system – and could therefore be used to analyse the system's structural capacity to respond to increased demand. A second map could show prices and number of actors at different points, and could be used to analyse the system's conduct: i.e. profit margins and possible competition problems.

In any case, the maps and text should concentrate on the key features (section 6.4) – e.g. bottlenecks and constraints – in the system that were caused by the crisis, and which are relevant to the response options recommended below.

Section 7: Key findings – results of the gap analysis and market analysis

This section should summarize the main insights and interpretations that you and the team have gained from the EMMA investigation. These are essentially the outputs of Steps 7 and 8: the answers to the key analytical questions.

The gap-analysis results will probably take the following form:

- a matrix that quantifies the priority needs for each target group and shows the total gap estimated for the target population (see Box 7.3 and section 7.3);
- information about the likely duration of gaps, the access constraints, and the preferences expressed by different target groups about the form of assistance that they need (section 7.4).

The market-analysis results will probably take the form of answers to the following questions.

- *How it was before:* a summary of the market system's baseline capacity and performance (section 8.3).
- *What has happened:* findings about the impact of the emergency on the market system; and in particular an analysis of supply-and-demand problems in the emergency-affected situation (section 8.4).
- *How it is likely to perform in future:* an appraisal of the system's capacity and potential to contribute to the emergency response defined by the gap analysis (section 8.5).

This prediction will be based on the emergency's impact on the market system; how well market actors are coping, and thus performing, compared with the baseline situation; and the scale of the challenge that the system faces in now responding to affected population's needs.

NOTE: an important element of this section is to highlight the gaps in your knowledge that are due, for example, to limited information / time / team analytic skills. What you don't know, but probably need to know, may be as important as what you do now understand.

Section 8: Main recommendations and conclusions

This section is basically a summary of the outputs from Step 9.

Response logic

Do the findings above essentially direct us towards a response that relies on the market system performing well (e.g. cash), or one that assumes that it cannot do so (e.g. relief)?

How feasible is it to change the market system's capabilities through supportive interventions? (section 9.2)

Response options

Advantages, disadvantages, and feasibility of the main candidates for response activities (section 9.7).

Response recommendations

Activities or combinations of activities that the EMMA team is proposing, including recommendations for further investigation and monitoring activities (section 9.8).

10.4 EMMA: a final word

Congratulations, you have reached the end of the emergency market-system mapping and analysis toolkit.

If you have been using the EMMA toolkit already in a crisis, I hope it has enabled you to understand the important market aspects of the situation at hand, and to translate this knowledge effectively into programme decision-making processes. If you are planning to use EMMA, I hope you feel encouraged and empowered to introduce these tools and concepts in future emergencies.

This toolkit stems from a growing recognition that market systems matter immensely to people affected by disasters and crises. They matter partly because markets can often supply critical goods and services efficiently in the immediate aftermath of a crisis. They also matter because people depend on market systems as sources of income and remuneration, both in the immediate context and in the longer term.

Awareness of the value of rapid market analysis in emergencies is related to the growth of cash responses to crises. Efforts to forge stronger links between emergency and development programmes will also increase the demand for EMMA. The challenge for humanitarian agencies and donors in the coming years will be to incorporate this type of analysis into their emergency assessment and planning processes as a norm.

Because EMMA tools are rough-and-ready, speed-orientated processes, the application of the EMMA toolkit is much more of an art than a science. EMMA tools will be adapted and tailored to the needs of each unique emergency context; and EMMA users will inevitably develop their own style of mapping and analysis as they gain experience and confidence.

As time goes by, EMMA users will benefit from sharing their experiences and results with each other. Therefore we intend to create a 'community of practice' for EMMA practitioners. This will have a home at www.emma-toolkit.info. The website will be a location for an on-line version of the toolkit and accompanying reference material. It will also be a place where EMMA users can post copies of EMMA reports for others to read, share experiences and lessons learned, and get advice.

Bibliography

All weblinks accessed 9 July 2009

ACF International Network (2007) *Implementing Cash-based Interventions: A Guideline for Aid Workers*, ACF Food Security Guideline, available from www.actionagainsthunger.org.uk/resource-centre/online-library/detail/media/implementing-cash-based-interventions-a-guideline-for-aid-workers/

Adams, L. (2007) *Learning from Cash Responses to the Tsunami, Final Report*, HPG Background Paper, Overseas Development Institute, London, available from www.odi.org.uk/hpg/papers/BGP_Tsunamilessons.pdf

Albu, M. and A. Griffith (2005) *Mapping the Market: A Framework for Rural Enterprise Development Policy and Practice*, Practical Action, Rugby, available from http://practicalaction.org/?id=mapping_the_market

Barrett, C., R. Bell, E. Lentz, and D. Maxwell (2009) 'Market information and food insecurity response analysis', *Food Security* 1: 151–168, Springer, Netherlands, available from www.springerlink.com/content/20t80w3656428335

Campbell, R. (2008) *Key Elements of the Value Chain Approach*, USAID Briefing Paper, available from www.microlinks.org/ev_en.php?ID=24002_201&ID2=DO_TOPIC

CMM (2005) *Livelihood and Conflict: A Toolkit for Intervention*, Office of Conflict Management and Mitigation, USAID, Washington, available from www.usaid.gov/our_work/cross-cutting_programs/conflict/publications/docs/CMM_Livelihoods_and_Conflict_Dec_2005.pdf

Creti, P. and S. Jaspars (2006) *Cash-transfer Programming in Emergencies*, Oxfam GB Publishing, available from http://publications.oxfam.org.uk/oxfam/add_info_024.asp

Donovan, C., M. McGlinchy, J. Staatz, and D. Tschirley (2005) *Emergency Needs Assessments and the Impact of Food Aid on Local Markets*, Desk review by Michigan University, for UN World Food Programme SENAC, Rome, available from http://documents.wfp.org/stellent/groups/public/documents/ena/wfp086537.pdf

FAO and ILO (2009) *The Livelihood Assessment Tool-kit: Analyzing and Responding to the Impact of Disasters on the Livelihoods of People*, FAO, Rome and ILO, Geneva, available from www.fao.org/fileadmin/templates/tc/tce/pdf/Livelihood_Assessment_Toolkit.pdf

FEG Consulting and Save the Children (2008) *The Practitioners' Guide to the Household Economy Approach*, Regional Hunger and Vulnerability Program, Johannesburg, available from www.feg-consulting.com/resource/practitioners-guide-to-hea

FEWS NET (2008) *Structure-Conduct-Performance and Food Security*, Markets Guidance No 2, USAID, Washington DC, available from http://pdf.usaid.gov/pdf_docs/PNADL965.pdf

Harvey, P. (2005) *Cash and Vouchers in Emergencies*, HPG discussion paper, Overseas Development Institute, London, available from www.odi.org.uk/resources/download/ 310.pdf

Harvey, P. (2007) *Cash-based Responses in Emergencies*, HPG briefing paper 25, Overseas Development Institute, London, available from www.odi.org.uk/resources/download/256.pdf

ICRC (2007) *Guidelines for Cash Transfer Programming*, ICRC and International Federation of Red Cross and Red Crescent Societies, Geneva, available from www.icrc.org/web/eng/siteeng0.nsf/html/publication-guidelines-cash-transfer-programming

Inter-Agency Standing Committee (2006) *Women, Girls, Boys and Men: Different Needs – Equal Opportunities. IASC Gender Handbook in Humanitarian Action*, UNHCR, available at www.unhcr.org/refworld/docid/46978c842.html

Jaspars, S. and D. Maxwell (2009) *Food Security and Livelihoods Programming in Conflict: A Teview*, HPN network paper 65, Overseas Development Institute, London, available from www.odihpn.org/documents/networkpaper065.pdf

Lor-Mehdiabadi, W. and A. Adams (2008) *Evaluation and Review of the Use of Cash and Vouchers in Humanitarian Crisis*, for European Commission (DG ECHO), available from http://ec.europa.eu/echo/files/policies/evaluation/2008/cash_review_report.pdf

Market Development Working Group (2007) *Market Development in Crisis-affected Environments: Emerging Lessons for Achieving Pro-poor Economic Reconstruction*, The SEEP Network, Washington, available from http://communities.seepnetwork.org/edexchange/node/276f

Mercy Corps (2007) *Guide to Cash-for-work Programming*, Mercy Corps, Portland, USA, available from www.mercycorps.org/publications/11913

Miehlbradt, A. and L. Jones (2006) *Market Research for Value Chain Initiatives*, MEDA, available from www.meda.org/WhatWeDo/ProductionMarketingLinkages/Resources/Publications.html

Moseley, K. and J. Bernson (2006) *Assessment of Emergency and Transition Situations (Assets Guidebook)*, Mercy Corps, Portland, USA, available from www.mercycorps.org/files/file1137799681.pdf

OFDA (2008) *Guidelines for Unsolicited Proposals and Reporting*, USAID, Washington DC, available from www.usaid.gov/our_work/humanitarian_assistance/disaster_assistance/resources/#grants

SEEP Network (2009) *Minimum Standards for Economic Recovery After Crisis*, The SEEP Network, Washington, available from http://communities.seepnetwork.org/econrecovery/node/821

Sperling, L. (2008) *When Disaster Strikes: A Guide to Assessing Seed System Security*, CIAT Publication 363, International Centre for Tropical Agriculture, Cali, Colombia, available from www.ciat.cgiar.org/africa/pdf/sssa_manual_ciat.pdf

Watson, C. and A. Catley (2008) *Livelihoods, Livestock and Humanitarian Response: The Livestock Emergency Guidelines and Standards*, HPN network paper 64, Overseas Development Institute, London, available from www.odihpn.org/documents/networkpaper064.pdf

WFP (2009) *Emergency Food Security Assessment Handbook*, 2nd edition, UN World Food Programme, available from www.wfp.org/content/emergency-food-security-assessment-handbook

Young, H., S. Jaspars, R. Brown, J. Frize, and H. Khogali (2001) *Food-security Assessments in Emergencies: A Livelihoods Approach*, HPN network paper 36, Overseas Development Institute, London, available from www.odihpn.org/documents/networkpaper036.pdf

Glossary

This glossary provides definitions for commonly used terminology in the EMMA toolkit. These definitions are based upon widely accepted definitions in work related to economic development, microfinance, enterprise development, livelihoods, market development, agriculture, and food security. Definitions are adapted from various sources, including the following:

- *Implementing Cash-based Interventions: A Guideline for Aid Workers* (ACF International Network, 2007);
- *The Practitioners' Guide to the Household Economy Approach* (FEG Consulting and Save the Children, 2008);
- *Women, Girls, Boys and Men: Different Needs – Equal Opportunities. IASC Gender Handbook in Humanitarian Action* (Inter-Agency Standing Committee, 2006);
- *Minimum Standards for Economic Recovery After Crisis* (SEEP Network, 2009).

Acceptable price rise. Price increases are often inevitable in an emergency situation – and do not necessarily indicate uncompetitive behaviour or poor conduct by market actors. Price rises are acceptable when they reflect genuinely higher costs or risks incurred by producers or traders. *See also* 'inflation'.

Access to markets. A measure of how many people (e.g. what proportion of a target population) can both afford to buy, and physically reach, a reliable supplier of a particular food stuff, non-food item, or service. The concept of access can also be applied to sellers, producers or labour in an income market system.

Aggregate demand/supply. The comprehensive total value of goods or services in a particular market. If not specified, it often refers to the national market.

Appropriate imprecision. An active strategy in data analysis to avoid spurious or unnecessary precision, being satisfied instead with adequate approximations and rough estimates. It means not spending so much time trying to achieve precision on one issue that you neglect others. It also means avoiding false precision – for example, giving a result as 23.7 per cent, when in reality we can only be sure that the answer is 'about a quarter'.

Asset protection. Most often refers to actions to help affected populations to avoid the sale or consumption of important natural or household assets. As well as cash transfers or relief distributions, asset protection may include activities to physically protect natural and household assets; to ensure access to communal assets; or to ensure that people's assets are not threatened by local laws or cultural norms.

Availability. A measure of the quantity (volume) of goods, food, or non-food items existing in a market system that can be mobilized to meet the needs of a target population within a particular time-frame. Availability is determined by considering production, imports, and stocks, along with the lead-times required to move these to where they are needed.

Barriers to entry. Obstacles in the path of any enterprise, producer, trader, or other market actor that make it difficult to fairly enter, engage in, or do business in a given market system. Barriers may include non-recoverable (sunk) investment costs, restrictive rules, regulations or trading practices, uncompetitive (predatory) pricing, intellectual-property rules, economies of scale, and customer loyalty to existing businesses.

Baseline. A measurement, calculation, or situation analysis that is used as a basis for comparison with the current or future situation. In EMMA, the baseline market map aims to represent a hypothetical 'what if the crisis had not occurred' situation, against which the impact of the emergency can be compared.

Bottleneck. Any effective constraint on the maximum speed or quantity of a production or trading activity – especially one which reduces the performance of the overall market system.

Business linkages (also known as 'market linkages'). Linkages refer to the trading relationships between and among producers, traders, and other enterprises in a supply chain or value chain.

Business services (also known as 'business development services', or BDS). The wide array of non-financial services that producers, traders, and other enterprises need in order to enter a market, survive, produce, compete, and grow. Examples include advice on planning, accountancy, bookkeeping, legal issues, marketing, product development, input supply, and equipment sale or leasing, as well as training for specific trades and providing access to improved technologies.

Cartel. A group of enterprises or traders who attempt to limit competition and control prices or the supply of a good or service through mutual restraint on production or supply, or simply by colluding to fix prices. *See also* 'oligopoly'.

Cash-based initiative. A general term for any type of humanitarian response involving the provision of cash or tokens (e.g. vouchers) to an emergency-affected population. Includes cash grants, cash-for-work, conditional cash transfers, repatriation and demobilization grants, and voucher programmes.

Cash grant/cash transfer. Provision of money to targeted households or persons, given without any requirement to work. Can be given as emergency relief, for support to livelihood recovery, or as a social safety net. *See also* 'conditional cash grant'.

Cash for work. Provision of temporary paid employment to targeted households or persons. As with grants, cash for work can be provided as emergency relief, in support of livelihood recovery, or as a social safety net.

Competition. Competition arises when there are a sufficient number of traders (sellers or buyers) vying with each other for business in a market, such that no single individual or enterprise dominates the market (*See* 'monopoly' and 'market power'). When there is effective competition, no-one can unfairly set the price of a good or service. This usually brings lower prices or better quality for consumers, or higher returns for producers and employees. Truly competitive markets also depend on traders being unable to collude among themselves to enforce a set price for goods *See* 'cartel'.

Competitiveness. This is a completely different concept from competition. It refers to the ability and performance of an individual enterprise (or an entire value chain) to out-sell and supply goods and/or services, compared with rivals in a given market.

Complex emergencies. A humanitarian crisis where there is total or considerable breakdown of authority resulting from internal or external conflict, and which requires an international response that goes beyond the mandate or capacity of any single agency or the on-going United Nations country programme.

Conditional cash transfer/grant. A cash grant whereby the recipient has to fulfil certain conditions, e.g. send children to school, plant seeds, build foundations for a house, demobilize.

Conduct (of market actors). The patterns of behaviour that traders and other market participants adopt to affect or adjust to the markets in which they sell or buy. These include price-setting behaviour, and buying and selling practices.

Connectedness. Describes the extent to which short-term emergency responses are planned and carried out in a way that takes into account the longer-term responses (reconstruction and development). The concept refers strictly to humanitarian contexts where true sustainability may not be possible.

Coping mechanism/strategy. When people's normal livelihood patterns or sources of income are disrupted by a crisis, the ways in which they change their economic behaviour are called their coping mechanisms (or coping strategies). Coping mechanisms are not used every year, but are the adaptation to a specific problem – e.g. reducing non-essential expenditure, eating wild foods, or adopting new ways of earning income. The concept applies equally well to households and other market actors such as producers, shop keepers, vendors, and traders. *See also* 'negative coping strategy'.

Corruption. The abuse of entrusted power for private gain, including financial corruption, such as fraud, bribery, and kick-backs. It also includes non-financial benefits such as the manipulation or diversion of humanitarian assistance to benefit non-target groups, or the allocation of relief resources in exchange for favours.

Cost-effective. Economical in terms of the ratio of tangible benefits achieved for money spent.

Critical market systems. The specific market systems that are most urgently relevant to the target population's emergency needs. Essentially those markets that had or could have a major role in ensuring survival or in protecting livelihoods of the target population.

Demand (also 'effective demand'). The amount (quantity) of a particular economic good, item, or service that a group of consumers (or buyers) will want to purchase at a given price. Consumers' (buyers') needs and desires must be accompanied by purchasing power (money) to be considered effective in the analysis of demand. Where lack of money is a significant constraint for the target population, the immediate result of cash-based initiatives is usually to increase effective demand.

Distress strategy (or 'survival strategy'). A distress, or survival, strategy is a way in which people adapt their economic behaviour in order to survive, but at the cost of long-term negative impacts on themselves – usually because they have failed to cope. Examples would be selling one's last productive assets, or cutting down on essential expenditure such as health care or education.

Economic growth. Increase in the capacity of a country or an economic region to produce goods and services. It also refers to the increase in market value of the goods and services produced by an economy. It is usually calculated using inflation-adjusted figures, in order to discount the effect of inflation on the price of the goods and services produced.

Effective demand. See 'demand'

Elasticity of demand. A measure of how sensitive to price changes is the quantity demanded by buyers or consumers. Goods on which people cut back sharply when prices rise or incomes are reduced (e.g. luxury items) have 'elastic demand'. Those that they continue to need and buy (e.g. staple foods) are said to have 'inelastic demand'. Goods in critical market systems usually fall into the second category.

Elasticity of supply. A measure of how sensitive to prices is the quantity supplied by producers or traders. Goods that can easily be supplied in greater quantities if prices rise have 'elastic supply'. Those that are difficult to quickly produce or import in greater volumes are said to have 'inelastic supply'. In emergency situations, elasticities are often unpredictable, due to disruption of supply chains.

Embedded services. Many informally provided services are 'embedded' freely within other trading relationships; e.g. shop keepers may allow their customers to take goods and pay later; inputs suppliers may provide free agricultural advice; traders may provide customer feed-back to small producers. This can be an indicator of a healthy and well-functioning market system.

Emergency situation. A situation with exceptional and widespread threats to life, health, and basic subsistence which are beyond the coping capacity of individuals and the community.

Enabling environment. An environment of policies, regulations, norms, institutions, and overall economic governance which allows market systems to function and perform well *See* 'performance'.

Enterprise. Any entity engaged in an economic activity, irrespective of its legal form. This includes self-employed persons, family businesses, partnerships, and group businesses (associations, co-operatives, informal groups) that are regularly engaged in an economic activity.

Enterprise development. Activities or programmes supporting the start-up and growth of private-sector businesses.

E.V.I. Acronym for 'extremely vulnerable individual'; for example: disabled, elderly, or sick adults, young children, and those who are traumatized or mentally unfit.

Extraordinary market system. A market system that did not function on a large scale before the crisis, but might now play an important role in meeting emergency needs.

Facilitator. A project or individual that gives indirect support to the actors in market systems. Rather than delivering support directly, a facilitator orchestrates interventions that build local capacity for providing services and/or solutions to recurrent constraints. Preferably this is done through existing business-service providers in the private sector.

Financial services. The wide array of formal and informal services used by households, producers, traders, and other enterprises in a market system. This includes savings, loans, insurance, remittances, and leasing services.

Formal sector/economy. This refers to enterprises and businesses that are licensed or registered, regulated, and (usually) taxed by the government *See* 'informal sector/ economy' in contrast.

Gender. Gender refers to the social differences between females and males that are learned and (though deeply rooted in every culture) are changeable over time. Gender differences have wide variations both within and between cultures. Along with class and race, they determine the roles, power, and resources of females and males in any society.

Gender analysis. Analysis that examines the relationships between females and males and their access to and control of resources, their roles, and the constraints that they face relative to each other. Gender analysis should be integrated into humanitarian needs assessments and all sector assessments or situational analyses, to ensure that gender-based injustices and inequalities are not exacerbated by humanitarian interventions, and that where possible greater equality and justice in gender relations are promoted.

Gender mainstreaming. A strategy for ensuring that women's as well as men's concerns and experiences are an integral dimension of the design, implementation, monitoring, and evaluation of legislation, policies, and programmes in all political, economic, and societal spheres. It is the process of assessing the implications for women and men of any planned action in all areas and at all levels, so that women and men benefit equally, and inequality is not perpetuated.

Group assets. Assets owned formally or informally by a group of individuals engaged together in a business or livelihood activity. Examples of typical group-managed assets include irrigation systems, agricultural machinery, packaging equipment, warehouses, and generators. Group asset transfers tend to be larger in scale (value and size) than individual asset transfers, thus additional attention prior to transfer must be given to evaluating local market impact and implications.

Household. A group of people, often family-related, each with different abilities and needs, who live together most of the time, contribute to a common economy, and share the food, essential resources, and other income generated by it.

Household economy. The sum of ways in which a household acquires its income, its savings, and asset holdings, and by which it meets its needs for food and non-food items.

Import parity price. A local price which is equivalent to the international market price for a commodity, but converted into local currency, plus in addition any transport, tariff, and other costs that the buyer would bear if importing.

Income (output) market system. In EMMA, this refers to market systems that provide sources of income for a target population, through sale of produce, labour, or other outputs. Sometimes also called 'output' markets. This distinguishes them from supplier (input) market systems which are a source of food, items, or services for a target population.

Indirect humanitarian responses. Humanitarian actions directed at traders, officials, policy makers, etc. which lead indirectly to benefits for the ultimate target population. For example: rehabilitation of key infrastructure or transport links; grants for local businesses to restore stocks or rehabilitate premises; technical expertise to local businesses or service providers.

Inflation. A persistent increase in the average price level in the economy. Inflation occurs when prices in general increase over time. This does not mean that all prices necessarily increase, or increase at the same rate, but only that average prices follow an upward trend. Price rises can be caused by emergency-related factors, but they may also be an underlying feature of an inflationary economy.

Inflation-adjusted prices. When prices are compared over time – for example, between baseline and emergency-affected situations – past prices may be adjusted by an inflation factor, to enable a more realistic comparison. This is necessary when inflation is an underlying feature of the economy. In hyper-inflationary economies, it may be necessary to convert local prices into equivalent prices in a stable international currency, in order to do realistic analyses of changes.

Informal sector/economy. The informal sector or economy refers to work that is not regulated or taxed by the government. In most countries it covers a multiplicity of activities and actors, including the self-employed, paid workers in informal enterprises, unpaid workers in family businesses, casual workers without fixed employers, and sub-contracted workers linked to formal or informal enterprises. *See* 'formal sector / economy'.

Institution. An established rule, norm, or way of doing something that is widely accepted throughout society. Institutions provide the rules and guidelines needed to carry out the day-to-day activities of our lives; the crucial structure of a society; and the framework within which economic activity takes place.

Integrated market system. See 'market integration'

Iteration/iterative. An analytical process – starting with a rough approximation and using the results of each iterative step as inputs for the next step – in which the same action is essentially repeated until a sufficiently accurate final result is obtained.

Key analytical question. In EMMA investigations, market systems are usually selected because people have specific ideas or expectations about the operational value that EMMA will add. 'Key analytical questions' frame these ideas, and thus help EMMA teams to keep them in mind throughout the process.

Key informant. Any individual in a community or society whose knowledge is especially relevant for the purpose of the assessment.

Livelihood. A livelihood is a way of making a living. It comprises capabilities, skills, assets (including material and social resources), and activities that people put together to produce food, meet basic needs, earn income, or establish a means of living in any other way.

Livelihood groups. Groups of households with similar food, income sources, and livelihood assets who are subject to similar risks. Livelihood groups may correspond with a particular geographical area; or they may be defined by other factors such as wealth, ethnicity, and type.

Livelihood strategies. The strategies that people employ in order to utilize and transfer assets to produce income today and deal with problems tomorrow. These strategies change and adapt in response to various shocks, external influences, institutional norms and rules, and other factors.

Livelihood zones. Geographical areas within which people share broadly the same patterns of access to food and income, and have similar access to markets.

Margin. The difference between an enterprise's net sales and the (input) costs of goods and services used to achieve those sales.

Market. Any formal or informal structure (not necessarily a physical place) in which buyers and sellers exchange goods, labour, or services for cash or other goods. The word 'market' can simply mean the place in which goods or services are exchanged. However, in EMMA, markets are defined by forces of supply and demand, rather than geographical location e.g. 'imported cereals make up 40 per cent of the market'.

Market actors. All the different individuals and enterprises involved in buying and selling in a market system, including producers, suppliers, traders, processors, and consumers.

Market chain. General term for a supply chain or a value chain: a sequence of market actors who buy and sell a product or item as it moves from initial producer to final consumer.

Market conduct. See 'conduct'

Market development. Market-development programmes seek to help micro- and small enterprises to participate in, and benefit more from, the existing and potential markets in which they do business (including input and support markets, as well as final markets). The ultimate goal of market-development programmes is to stimulate sustainable economic growth that reduces poverty—primarily by ensuring that small-enterprise owners and their employees take part in growth and reap higher rewards.

Market integration. A market system is integrated when linkages between local, regional, and national market actors are working well. In an integrated market system, any imbalance of supply and demand in one area is compensated for by the relatively easy movement of goods from other nearby and regional markets.

Market power See also 'monopoly' and 'cartel'. The ability of an enterprise, trader, or other market actor to alter the price of a good or service without losing all their customers, suppliers, or employees to their competitors. In an ideal, perfectly competitive market, market actors would have no market power. However, in the real world, barriers to entry, entrenched gender and social relations, collusion, and other anti-competitive forms of conduct often enable some market actors to dominate price negotiations.

Market structure. In economics, market structure describes whether a market is essentially characterized by competition, or oligopoly, or monopoly. The degree of rivalry among buyers and sellers in a market – and hence its structure – is determined by relatively stable features such as the number and size distribution of market actors, the degree of differentiation between them, the availability of market information, and the nature of barriers to entry.

Market system. The complex web of people, trading structures, and rules that determines how a particular good or service is produced, accessed, and exchanged. It can be thought of as a network of market actors, supported by various forms of infrastructure and services, interacting within the context of rules and norms that shape their business environment.

Market-system analysis. The process of assessing and understanding the key features and characteristics of a market system so that predictions can be made about how prices, availability, and access will develop in future; and (in the case of EMMA) decisions made about whether or how to intervene to improve humanitarian outcomes.

Market-system support. For the purposes of the EMMA toolkit, market-system support means any intervention or action aimed at improving the performance of a critical market system, other than direct assistance (cash-based or in-kind) provided to the target population.

Micro-enterprise. A very small enterprise, including small farms, having fewer than five or ten workers (definitions vary), including the micro-entrepreneur and any unpaid family workers. Usually assumed to be owned and operated by poor people in the informal sector.

Microfinance. The provision of financial services adapted to the needs of poor people, such as micro-entrepreneurs. Especially includes the provision of small loans, the acceptance of small savings deposits, and provision of payments services needed by micro-entrepreneurs and other people who may lack access to mainstream financial services.

Monopoly. A situation in which a single market actor controls all (or nearly all of) the market for a given type of product or service. This is an extreme form of market power. It can arise because of barriers which prevent other rival traders competing: e.g. high entry costs, government regulation, or coercion and/or corruption. *See also* 'oligopoly'.

Negative coping strategy (also known as 'distress strategy'). If coping strategies have long-term negative consequences, then people have failed to cope and are adopting 'distress strategies'. Common examples include reducing daily food intake and reducing household expenditures on medical care and education.

Oligopoly. A situation in which a small number of market actors controls all (or nearly all of) the market for a given type of product or service. This is a less extreme form of market power than monopoly. However, oligopolies can lead to monopoly-like situations if those few traders collude to set prices, rather than competing against each other.

Optimal ignorance. An active strategy in EMMA fieldwork to disregard non-essential or unnecessary detail. It means focusing attention on the most relevant elements of the market system: those that influence access and availability for the target population. This strategy requires continuous reflection on the degree to which the information being gathered is relevant to the key analytical questions.

Performance (of a market system). The extent to which a market system produced outcomes that are considered good or preferred by society. In EMMA, 'market performance' refers to how well the market system fulfils its role in meeting humanitarian objectives. Measures of performance include availability and quality of goods sold, their price levels and price stability in the short and long term, access for the target population, profit levels and long-term viability of market actors.

Price fixing. A situation where an individual market actor, or a group acting in collusion, is able to use their market power to push the price for a commodity or service above (or below) the price which would naturally emerge if there was freer competition between rivals.

Priority needs. Food, materials, and services that are required by a target population to achieve Sphere minimum standards in disaster response, and other essential items that women and men identify in early emergency needs assessments.

Producer groups. Individuals engaged in producing similar products who are organized to achieve economies of scale, and production or marketing efficiencies.

Purchasing power. The financial capability of a consumer or household to buy an item, commodity, or service. Increasing or restoring people's purchasing power is the main immediate objective of direct cash-based initiatives.

Reference period. A defined period to which the baseline information refers. In EMMA, the baseline reference period should be relevant to the timing or season of the emergency and planned response. For example, if planning food responses during the next three-month growing season, the best baseline reference period may be the same three-month season last year.

Remittances. The earnings sent by migrants to their relatives in countries or communities of origin. In many communities, remittances constitute a significant and critical source of income at both local and national levels.

Responsive (functioning) market system. A market system that will respond well to higher effective demand by increasing supplies without excessive accompanying increases in prices.

Seasonal calendar. A graphical presentation of the months in which cultivation of food and cash crops, and other production or earning activities, take place. Seasonal calendars can show when food and other inputs are purchased, and key seasonal periods such as the rains, and periods of peak illness and hunger. They can be used to highlight other seasonal variations in market systems, such as changes in road access, costs of transport, and demand for casual labour.

Shock. Sudden, irregular events that significantly affect a household's or enterprise's ability to generate income by regular means. At the level of an economy or market, a shock is an event that disrupts established trading patterns and trends.

Social protection. Policies and plans that reduce economic and social vulnerability of poor and marginalized groups through transfer of food, cash, and other benefits.

Stocks. The stores or stockpiles of food or other items that are held by different market actors along a supply chain or value chain. *See* 'availability'.

Sub-sector. In enterprise development, a sub-sector is defined as all the enterprises and other market actors that buy and sell from each other in order to supply a particular set of products or services to final consumers *See* 'value chains'.

Subsidized sales. A market-support action in which traders or service providers receive a grant (e.g. to cover transportation costs, or re-stocking) on condition that they reduce their selling prices by an appropriate amount. It is appropriate only when prices are too high but there is no evidence that this is due to abuse of market power.

Supply chain. The sequence of market actors who buy and sell a commodity, product, or item as it moves from initial producers via processors and traders to final consumers. In EMMA, the term 'supply chain' is used particularly when the final consumers are the target population for humanitarian assistance. *See* 'value chain' in contrast.

Supply (input) market system. In EMMA, this refers to market systems which supply food, essential items, assets, or other inputs to a target population. Sometimes also called 'input' markets. This distinguishes them from income (output) market systems, which are a source of income for a target population.

Sustainability. A measure of whether an activity or intervention, and its longer-term impact, will continue after external funding has been withdrawn. It implies that local capacity to address recurring constraints exists or will be developed.

Target population. The mass of emergency-affected women, men, and children who it is intended should ultimately benefit from the emergency response. Usually, these are the most vulnerable or severely affected individuals and households in a disaster area. Often the target population is disaggregated into more clearly defined target groups with different situations and needs. Note: indirect humanitarian responses may involve assistance to market actors who are not part of the target population.

Trade volume. The volume (quantity) of food, goods, or items being produced or traded at a particular point in a market system. EMMA refers to estimates of 'production and trade' volumes, so as to include in the overall picture food or other goods that are produced for own consumption, but not traded.

Value chain. The sequence of market actors who buy and sell a commodity, product, or item as it moves from initial producers via processors, traders, and distributors to final consumers. In EMMA, the term 'value chain' is used particularly when the target population for humanitarian assistance are the producers or workers. *See* 'supply chain' in contrast.

Value-chain analysis. A type of market-system analysis which focuses on the dynamics of linkages within a productive sector, especially the way in which firms and countries are globally integrated. It includes a description of actors in the value chain and an analysis of constraints along the chain. It also considers dynamics (trends over time), and it does not limit itself to national boundaries.

Voucher. Vouchers are tokens or coupons issued by an agency or government which can be exchanged for a fixed set of goods, or goods up to a fixed sum of money, at certain shops or by certain traders. The agency which issued the vouchers then takes the vouchers handed back by the shops or traders in exchange for an agreed sum of money. They may be valid for several months, or only a particular market day ('fair').

Wealth group. A group of households within the same community who share similar capacities to exploit the different food and income options within a particular livelihood zone. These capacities determine a 'wealth status', indicated by measures such as, for example, whether the household's children go to school; whether the household can afford medical care; the size of their land; and whether or not they own livestock.

Index

Oxfam GB is a development, relief, and campaigning organization that works with others to fi nd lasting solutions to poverty and suffering around the world. Oxfam GB is a member of Oxfam International.
As part of its programme work, Oxfam GB undertakes research and documents its programme and humanitarian experience. This is disseminated through books, journals, policy papers, research reports, and campaign reports which are available for free download at: www.oxfam.org.uk/publications
www.oxfam.org.uk
Email: publish@oxfam.org.uk
Tel: +44 (0) 1865 473727
Oxfam House
John Smith Drive
Cowley
Oxford, OX4 2JY

For the past 75 years the **International Rescue Committee** has been at the forefront of humanitarian initiatives to assist people uprooted by war, persecution, or civil conflict – bringing them from **Harm to Home.**

www.theirc.org

InterAction is the largest coalition of U.S.-based international nongovernmental organizations (NGOs) focused on the world's poor and most vulnerable people. At InterAction, we recognize that our global challenges are interconnected and that we can't tackle any of them without addressing all of them. That's why we create a forum for leading NGOs, global thought leaders and policymakers to address our challenges collectively. Leveraging our shared expertise, on-the-ground insights from our 180 member organizations and strategic analyses of the foreign aid budget, we deliver a bold, new agenda to end global poverty and deliver humanitarian aid in every developing country.